IPD

~~SECRET~~ **DECLASSIFIED**

Instructions for the safeguarding, handling and transmission, storage, reproduction, change of classification, and accounting for SECRET material are described in AFR 205-1. Compliance with these instructions is mandatory.

CAUTION

This Document contains information affecting the National Defense of the United States. Its Transmission or the disclosure of its contents in any manner to an unauthorized person is prohibited and may result in severe criminal penalties under applicable Federal laws.

Individuals who have read the contents of the accompanying document will affix their signatures below.

AGENCY	NAME AND GRADE	DATE	AGENCY	NAME AND GRADE	DATE
AFCRB-73	*[signature]*	12 Dec			
AFCFSC?	*[signature]*	5 March		*AFR 205-1 April 3 9-30-61*	
AFOFS	*[signature]*				

~~SECRET~~

15AF 17 AUG 53 159 TEMP

AIR FORCE - HQ - ???

Happy Reading Comrad!
To Sviatoslav Liapunov
[signature] Ed D. P?t?r?

SILENT HEROES
OF THE COLD WAR

DECLASSIFIED

The mysterious military plane crash on a Nevada mountain peak — and the families who suffered an abyss of silence for generations.

Kyril D. Plaskon

Stephens Press · Las Vegas, Nevada

About the Cover
The photo is an Air Force image taken during the original recovery mission of the crash on Mount Charleston in 1955. This photo was given by the Air Force to Herbert E. Dobberstein, a member of a later demolition team. Before his death, he donated the images to the Atomic Testing Museum in Las Vegas; this image and many more were provided as a courtesy of the museum.

Designer: Sue Campbell
Editor: Jami Carpenter
Contributing Editor: Steven Ririe
Publishing Coordinator: Stacey Fott

Cataloging-in-Publication

Plaskon, Kyril D.
 Silent heroes of the Cold War declassified : the mysterious military plane crash on a Nevada mountain peak—and the families who endured an abyss of silence for a generation / Kyril D. Plaskon.
 204 p. : photos. ; 23 cm.
 Includes bibliographical references.
 An account of the 1955 airplane crash on Mt. Charleston, Nevada, that devastated the U-2 development program and of the efforts by the government to keep the information classified.

ISBN: 1-932173-60-9
ISBN-13: 978-1-932173-60-4

1. Airplanes, Military—Accidents. 2. Aircraft accidents—Investigations—Nevada. 3. U-2 (Reconnaissance aircraft). 3. Silent Heroes of the Cold War (Organization). I. Title.

363.12'456'0973 dc22   2008
2008932315

STEPHENS PRESS, LLC
A Stephens Media Company

Post Office Box 1600
Las Vegas, NV 89125-1600
www.stephenspress.com

Printed in the United States of America

*To my father, Daniel Stephen Plaskon,
who selflessly dedicates his life to
accountability in the aerospace industry
from Earth to Mars.*

*To my mother, Sandra Bovee, who
dedicates her life to education and
despises hypocrisy in government and
personal life.*

MISSIONS

Preface

Silent Heroes of the Cold War is the name of an organization created as a direct result of the discovery of the declassified documents. Its members spent a decade collecting information on the accident and contacting the victims' families. Today they are dedicated to creating a national memorial to commemorate the victims of this accident and all Cold War heroes.

The Silent Heroes of the Cold War Memorial Committee would like to extend our sincere appreciation for the financial support from the following donors:

DIAMOND DONORS

The Kreimendahl Family

Dwight & Barbara G. Mikel of the John Gaines Family

Terence O'Donnell's family thanks both God for the Silent Heroes, who helped preserve our freedom, and the Silent Heroes of the Cold War Memorial Committee for drawing attention to the price our Heroes paid for our freedom.

The Grace S. O'Donnell family.
Grace is the mother of Terence O'Donnell

GOLD DONORS

Mr. & Mrs. Roy Silent Rieber

Jo-Lynne Atkins & Alan Stoffregen of the George Pappas Family

Joy Cunniff Family daughter of Richard Hruda

Chase & Kelli Jackson

Mount Charleston Lodge

ACKNOWLEDGEMENTS

Thank you to all the families of the victims who found the courage to tell their stories, and to Steve and Julie Ririe, who thought these stories should be unearthed. Without them, this book would not have been possible.

I am grateful to my wife, Mina, and Mina's mother, Guler, who helped care for our daughter Alara while I worked on this project after Alara was born. Thank you to Art from the Heart, the shop that provided a bottomless cup of coffee and a seat from which to write away from the distractions of home.

FOREWORD

A nation reveals itself not only by the men it produces but also by the men it honors, the men it remembers.

—PRESIDENT JOHN F. KENNEDY

Some things never change. One such constant is government secrecy. Sometimes secrecy in government work is necessary and ultimately beneficial. Sometimes it is not. In every case it comes at a price.

A nation suffers when its government obscures its operations with a veil of secrecy. This suffering is especially acute for those who work behind that veil. Secret operations by their very nature require an absence of oversight, heightening the risk of bad decisions and flawed policies. Secrecy also obscures the achievements and sacrifices of a host of patriots who deserve to be acknowledged and honored. In many instances men and women are not commemorated for their achievements while they are alive, and their sacrifice goes unnoticed when they give their lives in the line of duty. Secrecy also impacts the families of America's covert heroes. While patriotic Americans serve secretly, their families suffer from never knowing the accomplishments of their loved ones. And should these covert heroes perish, their families are rarely provided with the information required for closure and peace.

No matter how great the sacrifices that this nation asks of its citizens, there will always be men and women who are willing to face the dangers and embrace the challenges of covert work.

Never has service in secrecy been more prevalent than

during the Cold War—the most dangerous conflict in our nation's history. During that 50-year stand-off, our nation's technological superiority helped us to prevail over our enemies. This superiority was only possible because of the high priority our nation placed on keeping its research and development secret, and because of the thousands who were willing to toil in obscurity to ensure that liberty prevailed.

Secrecy and patriotism were key ingredients in the creation of America's greatest intelligence advantage of the era. The U-2 spy plane—a project critics said was impossible—was unparalleled in its ability to gather intelligence. As a testament to the importance of this project, the plane remains a vital component of our reconnaissance forces throughout the world. While secrecy was crucial to the success of the U-2 project, it was also the source of the project's greatest tragedy.

On November 17, 1955, fourteen men assigned to the U-2 project made the ultimate sacrifice for their nation when their C-54 cargo plane crashed into Mount Charleston—a 12,000 foot mountain, ten miles from Las Vegas. No person is responsible for the deaths of these patriots. Imprudent shortcuts, a lack of oversight, and bureaucratic confusion—all symptoms of the dark side of government secrecy—combined to take the lives of these fourteen men and destroy their families.

It was, perhaps, a tragic necessity that these fourteen heroes were not honored immediately after the accident. Similarly, for a time some say it was prudent not to inform the men's families of the roles they played in the U-2 project. However, it is inexcusable that, once the project became less sensitive and the U-2 files were declassified, these heroes were not honored and their families were never notified of the extent and value of their service.

Thanks to Steve Ririe and Kyril Plaskon, we now have an opportunity to redeem the mistakes of the past. By finally telling their stories, we can in some way repay those who gave so much when our need for them was greatest. This is an important issue to me, not just as an American, but also as a Nevadan. From nuclear testing to air combat training, Nevada played a key role in the technological research that allowed us to win the Cold War. Nevada also played an important role in the development and testing of the U-2. And, sadly, Nevada was also the state in which the fourteen men who are the subject of this book lost their lives.

In telling the untold stories of fourteen silent heroes of the Cold War, this book is a monument to these patriots and their families, as well as to the hundreds of Nevadans and thousands of Americans who worked, lived, and died in obscurity beside them.

In reading this book, we are reminded not only of our duty to honor those who sacrificed on our behalf, but also of our duty to learn from our history. Keeping in mind the price of secrecy—a price made all too apparent in this book—we must learn to recognize when secrecy and sacrifice are necessary and when there are other paths to the same end. And when embracing secrecy is our only option, we must remember to embrace it with resignation and caution.

—Senator Harry Reid

INTRODUCTION

A Non-violent Weapon

A weapon that makes others look like child's play was first detonated by the United States at 5:29 a.m. on July 16, 1945, in Alamogordo, New Mexico. It's a good thing no human was in range. At ground zero an unfathomable heat melted the dirt into radioactive glass. A blinding flash lit up the sky. From a safe distance onlookers could see the white plume of fall-out rise in a towering mushroom cloud to neck-craning altitudes. The sound bellowed and the tremble registered on distant continents. Less than a month later, two of these bombs were used to kill more than 120,000 Japanese in an instant.

As if that weren't testimony enough to its power, in the decades that followed hundreds of these explosions rocked the Nevada Test Site, ninety miles northwest of Las Vegas. This was also a powerful promotional tool for Las Vegas. To draw tourists, the emerging, world-renowned city encouraged word to leak out about when each "secret" explosion would take place. Crowds of tourists and locals would gather at Mount Charleston to hear the rumble, feel the power and fear course through their bodies, and watch the enormous clouds of deadly dust rise and drift away in silence. Long after the visitors were gone, the radioactive fallout spread into the atmosphere every which way. It would often envelop Mount Charleston like a blanket on the very ground where the unsuspecting audiences had gathered.[1]

Four years after America's first explosion, Russia began its path of decimation with its first detonation of a nuclear device. The arms race was on. This was beyond the rattling of sabers. The thunderous test explosions filled the sky with mushroom clouds as superpowers pounded their soil like gorillas beating their chests — messages across continents between unofficial enemies. Americans who lived through it say it was like two men standing in a pool of gasoline, neck-deep, fighting over who had more matches. Igniting just one of the many matches they were feverishly amassing could annihilate them both and alter the world as they knew it. This was their world.

As the years wore on, the enthusiasm and awe of these weapons gave way to an increasing awareness that these explosions on what was, and remains to this day, a remote plot of land were one thing; but if these monsters were unleashed in the world's cities, the heat and rain of fallout could erase untold numbers of lives. We had already witnessed what would happen.

Admiration of these weapons turned to fear, becoming a part of how Americans lived their lives, from school bomb-raid drills to home fallout plans. My father was among them, having built a makeshift bomb shelter and amassed food rations. He told me his plan. If the world broke out into nuclear war and a bomb hit San Diego, he hoped it would only take three days for the fall-out to reach our farm in Potrero, California. We would drain our concrete pool, cover it with telephone poles and plywood and lock ourselves inside the makeshift cave with the food and port-a-potty until the danger had passed. His friends in the aerospace industry even came to see his plan and made a pact with him to join us in the shelter if need be.

For a decade, this terrifying arms race deadlocked our rival nations. So impenetrable were the Soviet Union's secrets that the United States coined it the "Iron Curtain." The only information that was willingly, enthusiastically, and widely disseminated by each side was the ferocious rate of building these deadly nuclear weapons. The Soviet Communist Party leaders boasted that behind Russia's Iron Curtain was a huge arsenal of nuclear weapons and long-range bombers with which to deliver them. But was the Soviet bark worse than the bite?

What our nation needed was a new weapon, one that could derail the two superpowers and our people from the rush down the path to nuclear annihilation. That disarming weapon was an unlikely one. It was information, and its acquisition could not be gained with brute force.

Trying to get this information was more than tough. Up to this point, most of the nation's information about the Soviet Union had been acquired through the interrogation of German World War II prisoners returning from Russia. As time passed, the information was outdated and the source itself was also drying up. So in the 1940s the Air Force and Navy attempted aerial photography of the Soviet Union. US aircraft were outfitted with radar-detecting devices and when a hole in the Soviet Union's air warning network was detected, the pilots would dart in and take photographs. But in the 1950s, the Soviets began aggressively defending their airspace, attacking numerous US, British, and Turkish aircraft. Even so, the US wasn't about to abandon the idea of aerial photography.

President Dwight D. Eisenhower felt he had no choice but to do everything in his power to learn the truth about what was behind that Iron Curtain. The CIA determined that the only way to find out was to develop a plane like no other. It would have to fly through the earth's stratosphere in the highest of the earth's clouds, at least 60,000 feet above the earth, hopefully beyond the capabilities of Soviet defenses. It would have to be capable of flying 1,500 nautical miles carrying a 500 pound high-resolution, large format camera to take pictures of the reality on enemy ground. Many aeronautic engineers called it impossible.

This tool was only a concept. This would be the secret card in the US's sleeve in what was the highest stakes poker game of posturing and bluffs, a poker game where each side horded secrets and worked relentlessly to uncloak the other. Winner would take all.

On this mission, the CIA chose to enter into a contract with a company called Lockheed, the premiere aerospace company at the time. Not only was the plane to be top-secret, but also there needed to be a top-secret airbase at which to test it. That was something California didn't have, and while the company's development operations were in California, the testing would have to take place somewhere else. To the public, the aircraft did not exist and neither did the airstrip where the plane would be tested. The CIA called it the "U-2" and the secret airbase was commonly known as "Area 51," "Watertown," and "Groom Lake."

Once the U-2 was shaping into reality, it was not an easy matter for President Eisenhower to approve actually using it for surveillance flights over this undeclared enemy's territory. In 1955, he said:

Well, boys, I believe the country needs this information,

and I'm going to approve it. But I tell you one thing.
Some day one of these machines is going to be caught,
and we're going to have a storm.

At the time of the development of the U-2, there was no greater top secret or "black project" in the United States. Secrecy was believed to be paramount to its success and few outside the project knew much about it. Little did we know, the path of secrecy was also paved with corpses, casualties of many classified U-2 missions. The military and CIA determined that the success of these missions depended on keeping even the casualties quiet, even if dead men tell no tales.

The entire mission of the U-2 was not declassified until 1998. That same year the CIA published *The CIA and the U-2 Program*, a book that was initially labeled as "secret," too. Names and locations were even redacted in the declassified document, but still the book explained how a unique classified flight started between Burbank and Area 51 on the development missions of the U-2. According to the text, in 1955 the deliveries of U-2 airframes to the test site in Nevada increased, creating a major logistical problem: how to bring Lockheed employees from Burbank to the secret airbase without raising a lot of curiosity about what strange thing was going on in this desolate plot of Nevada desert. The decision was made to bring employees to the site only twice a week, every Monday and Friday. Despite the desire for ultimate secrecy and keeping the flights to a minimum, flights only twice a week weren't sufficient for the size of the project. According to the CIA, daily flights soon began carrying essential personnel, supplies, visitors, and contractors. These flights began on October 3, 1955, on what became known as "Bissell's Narrow-Gauge Airline." Only a few weeks after the flights started, one exploded on the peak of Mount Charleston, killing the CIA's Project Security Officer for this entire secret mission. The CIA called this event "the greatest single loss of life in the entire U-2 program."

No one knew the U-2 existed, but on that tragic day in the infancy of the project, that secret was nearly revealed. In these pages are the incredible stories of how a project was kept secret and how it affected the families of fourteen victims. The victims included the private industry U-2 developers, flight crew and CIA security.

These unheralded victims and their brain trust were a loss in the nation's secret arsenal, our best weapon in the Cold War. They engaged in what was largely a war of information, a unique war, not one of muscle but of mind. Their mission was one of many that helped America cut through the Iron Curtain and eventually led to the end of the Cold War.

Sadly, by the time the official truth was revealed with the declassification of the U-2 project documents in 1998, it was too late for many of the victims' families. They died never knowing the honorable work of their loved ones. For the family members who are still alive, the truth brings recognition and heroism that could never come too late.

CHAPTER I

Destination Classified

Burbank, California was exploding with aerospace engineers, pilots, and military-funded projects in 1955, where some of the most exciting industry work of the time had just begun to take flight. While the origins were in Burbank, the location where the work was coming to fruition was a world away in Nevada on a tiny dry lakebed in a state where the Feds are the authority over more than 80 percent of the land.

To this little-known point in the desert a small group of men were headed at 6:13 a.m. on November 17, 1955. Military Air Transport System, Classified Missions Pilot George Pappas prepared to leave from the Lockheed Air Terminal in Burbank on a routine flight for that secret lakebed. His destination was listed as Watertown.

Shortly before sunrise passengers climbed aboard Pappas' flight, a DC4/C-54. The plane was United States Air Force 9068 with red wing tips and tail.

The scheduled flight departure was 7:00 a.m., but one of the passengers hadn't shown up, so Pappas waited. Eventually the hatch closed and the C-54's four propel-

Passengers in Burbank, California climb aboard a C-54.

Courtesy of Silent Heroes of the Cold War Corporation

lers cut through the air. Wind billowed over the metallic skin as the pilot released the brake. The wheels lurched forward and USAF 9068 began to taxi down the tarmac.

To most people, nothing would have seemed out of the ordinary about this plane, one of many taking off that day in Burbank. But while unremarkable on the outside, the growl of these engines was the roar of the nation's safest, most efficient and renowned military workhorses. On this day the plane was pursuing another of the many military missions this model had successfully accomplished, missions that have cemented this aircraft's uncelebrated place in American history.

The C-54 is considered to have played an unsung role in wresting victory from the Axis during WWII. For its prowess in that war, the US Air Force dubbed the C-54, "Skymaster." Its four powerful 1,200 horsepower engines were proven in WWII as astoundingly reliable, gaining the unchallenged respect of maintenance crews. This model was tremendously versatile. It could haul 16,000 pounds of dead weight on round-the-clock missions as it did during the Berlin Airlift, and it could do it through the most arduous weather conditions and navigational obstacles.

On some missions the Skymaster also carried the most precious of live cargo. President Franklin D. Roosevelt used it, making the C-54 the first presidential aircraft. Roosevelt's model was called a C-54C and was nick-named "Sacred Cow." It included a special electric wheel-chair lift for the president. But by carrying the president, the C-54 also became the first in a line of what we now call "Air Force One."

Lockheed also custom built a C-54 for Winston Churchill. His Skymaster was outfitted for both luxury and practicality. It included heavy armor to shield him in the event of a fighter attack so that he would be protected, even while he used the luxurious electrically-heated toilet seat.

Some C-54 models could thermally de-ice their wings as well, a state of the art idea at the time. Over the years the C-54 was adapted to carry enormous under-wing radio and radar gear. Such a versatile aircraft was destined to evolve from military to business use, from carrying paratroopers to civilian international travelers. By the 1960s, the C-54 was adapted to carry eighty-five passengers and was used daily by no less than four airlines in eighteen countries.

But on this day in 1955, this pilot in Burbank on his way to Watertown would have only been aware of his craft's accomplishments to date. He knew that during WWII, pilots in the C-54 took daily risks that would seem frightful in any other aircraft, but he wasn't concerned. Its single tail wing design and tremendously powerful engines allowed pilots to frequently dismiss bad weather.[2]

It would seem like nothing could damn this plane; and it was with that confidence that on the 17th day of November 1955, with what seemed to be just another crew, the C-54 "officially" cleared for lift-off just before sunrise. Its unique tail number, like a license plate, was a blur in the early morning light: USAF 9068.

Unlike this plane's civilian counterparts at the same airport, when USAF 9068 finally left the tarmac, it didn't rise far into the sky. It flew low and careened quickly toward the mountains, then behind those mountains, and out of sight. The order was to fly low, below the cover of intermittent 10,000 foot mountains that stood in the distance, standard for these top-secret military flights to Watertown.

An Artist rendering of USAF 9068.

Courtesy of Silent Heroes of the Cold War Corporation

Some believe the windows of the plane were blacked out so that not even the passengers knew where they were going, but frequent passengers say they had a clear view of the brown desert below, entirely devoid of landmarks. There was simply nothing to see out the windows other than barren western desert as far as the eye could see, so what good would it really do to hide it from the passengers. The passengers likely paid little attention and joked and enjoyed their trip to an amazing project that was deserving of national pride.

Weather reports that day showed that tailwinds of 50-60 knots would have helped the C-54 ascend and cross hundreds of miles over the hills and jagged unforgiving rocks as it cut northeast through the clear and empty Mojave desert. Weather reports also showed that following close behind this lonely plane, somewhere to the northwest, was a storm, a challenge which the C-54 rarely saw. This silent enormous storm was riding the wind, too, edging closer and towering behind them toward the same destination.

About thirty minutes after take-off, the plane and its crew crossed the unmarked California/Nevada state line and cruised over a beacon station at the dusty mining town of Goodsprings, Nevada. There the crew changed not only direction, but flight status. They went silent, cutting contact with air traffic controllers, barreling into the abyss of air to the north on their own. Using only "visual means" ensured that their path was protected from any prying enemies that might want to track it as they plowed toward Watertown.

As the pilot veered the controls north under the new visual-only flight status, he could only see the world ahead through the small cockpit window. With no other means for monitoring the world around him, the pilot was oblivious to the approaching storm or the challenge that lay ahead. As the plane took a turn north over Goodsprings, a strong tailwind suddenly became a crosswind pushing them off course to the east.

At an altitude of around 9,000 feet, there shouldn't have been much to worry about, but then the scenery began to change. The mountains kept rising out of the desert toward the plane. As the plane continued north, giant gray swaths of clouds began to build over the steep hills of the Spring Mountain Range momentarily occluding the view. Flying by sight through a storm in the mountains was not part of the plan.

The C-54 careened along the Las Vegas side of the Spring Mountains, temporarily shielded by the cliffs that faced the dimming morning lights of the Las Vegas valley.

With its powerful wall of wind and freezing water spilling around the mountain range and across the flatlands to the north, the storm raced across the desert and low foothills until it also reached the desolate dry lakebed hundreds of miles away that was Watertown. There, the storm hailed ferociously, kicking up near hurricane-force winds.

Meanwhile, the disoriented crew of the C-54 were dodging peaks just above the tree and snow-covered mountain range when their normal flight path should have taken them over flat desert.

Only a half hour after they had left the safety of the ground, the danger was obvious. The pilot broke the coveted radio silence and tried to call his destination, not once, but desperately every five minutes. No response. The wild terrain blocked their radio signals. By virtue of their mission, these men weren't supposed to be there in the first place, and they weren't the responsibility of any airport that would have heard them calling somewhere out there in the darkening skies.

Staff Sergeant Alfred Arneho was working in the control tower at Nellis Air Force Base that morning. Every morning this detail-oriented airman liked to have a piece of paper in front of him to record the transmissions as flights took off. He overheard an unusual transmission from the C-54. Little did Arneho know, it was a pilot breaking radio silence. Even though the C-54 flight wasn't on his schedule, he jotted it down out of habit. He

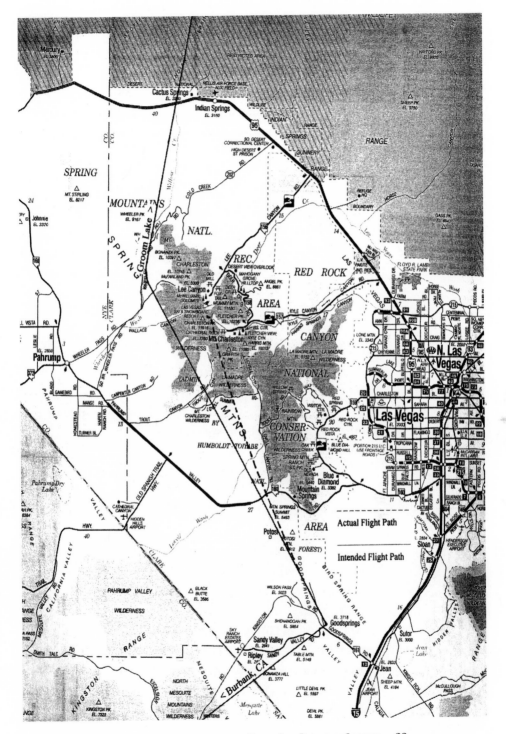

thought the pilot of the C-54 sounded calm when calling for Watertown and Indian Springs towers.

Arneho heard the C-54 pilot's high-frequency transmission sometime between 8:08 and 8:20 a.m. Arneho didn't respond because he assumed the pilot was communicating with Indian Springs. Five minutes later he heard the same pilot call for Indian Springs again. By that time, however, Sergeant Arneho was swamped and had to tend to his own traffic at Nellis Air Force Base.

As the C-54 battled its way north through the mountains and clouds, the peaks loomed taller and closer, rising along sides of the plane. Finally a clearing in the clouds appeared and mountains seemed to open.

On a clear day, visitors to Kyle Canyon can see the terrain. It's a horseshoe-shaped valley surrounded by cliffs that rise nearly 10,000 feet high on all sides, but this view would have been blurred when the C-54 crossed the canyon at speeds of more than 200 knots.

The plane and its crew were in a rocky and treacherous world, careening through the air with the solid walls of the canyon keeping the air traffic controllers who could save them oblivious to the peril the C-54 faced.

With no one on the ground to guide them, the mountain terrain continued to close in, and the storm grew more violent. Every passing second they survived seemed a miracle as the crew dodged the rising peaks in a combination of guesswork, expertise, and intuition. Every minute they hoped something would bring them closer to contact with the world around them without compromising the classified mission.

After passing Griffith Peak, the mountains disappeared from view, and a puff of clouds filled the sky above Kyle Canyon. There was only one way out. In a seeming moment of clarity and calculation, the pilot turned west back toward the original planned flight path.

At that moment, the C-54 and its precious crew were aimed dead center at the highest peak in all of the surrounding Spring Mountain Range. The treeless, rocky, snow-covered gray mound was in a shower of snow as the giant storm poured over the top of it.

On all sides, the unfamiliar range of cliffs was closing in through the cockpit glass; dark gray cliffs jutted hundreds of feet above them only a breath away. Radio signals turned to white noise. The white peak suddenly appeared, filling the pilot's entire view. The passengers were now in a seemingly windowless tube, plowing up through the violent weather. They felt the extreme force of the plane's acceleration as the pilot's instinct took hold. He gripped the controls and pulled the yoke back and shoved the throttle forward, sending the machine up against the downward force of the immense storm pouring over the mountain onto them. With the passing of every millisecond, the snow on this solid mountain began to swallow them.

Visitors to Mount Charleston Lodge Resort a few thousand feet below could hear the struggling aircraft. The echo of the four engines' roar filled the valley like a suffocating wall of noise as the pilot pressed the throttle to maximum speed.

The unsuspecting tourists on the ground below craned their necks toward the deafening inescapable sound that was erupting in the early morning. Witnesses said they saw the silvery bird cut through the clouds for an instant and then disappear back into the fog just before 8:30 a.m.

The rocky soil of Mount Charleston was close enough to touch the plane as the pilot used the craft's tremendous force to lift it and split its way through the storm that was pounding them. At 11,300 feet the pilot hoped there were only another few feet to clear the peak. Then the barren and rocky earth touched them. The pilot strong-armed the controls and launched the plane into the air again, through the frigid thin air for another 60 feet before stalling. The roaring engines gave way to the weight of the moaning wind. The right propeller dug into the mountain; the pilot frantically jammed the controls to the left hoping to keep it afloat, but it was too late. The left wing and propeller met with the mountain, snapping it off instantly. The nose of the plane flattened into the mountain. The fuselage cracked in two, throwing the crew and passengers through the plane and out into the beautiful and deadly wasteland. In an instant, this classified mission was a crushed pile of burning rubble. The tail of the plane smashed down onto the icy peak, sliding another twenty feet and then spilling weak cries of smoke and fire into the wild, desolate air.

When the storm had passed, Las Vegas saw a curious glow in the distant sky, right where the mountain was located. The next morning, in the cool air of Henderson, Nevada, ten miles southeast of Las Vegas, Laverne Hanks remembers it like it was yesterday:

"Flame, just like there was a fire," the 80-year-old recalled.

There, on top of that distant peak was a plume of smoke. Little did she know, her brother's body was there, lifeless in the swirling and freezing wind.

It wasn't long before the Hanks family found out their relative was on that plane. Laverne recalled that her husband tried desperately to get up to the base of the mountain.

It happened on a Thursday night. Friday morning, my husband was up on Mount Charleston.

All the TV networks were there at the base, she said. Her husband tried in his headstrong way to drive up the mountain with a CBS crew, but they were stopped miles away at the entrance of Highway 158.

"The man standing there with the rifle, he said 'you cross this line, I will shoot you.' My husband was followed all the way home by the FBI." Armed military police blocked the way, indefinitely sealing the only road to and from the mountain to ensure that the top-secret cargo was secure. Whether it was the FBI that followed Hanks or not, this was the first in a long line of unsuccessful attempts to eliminate the burning questions: "What happened?" and "Why did they die?"

CHAPTER II

Salvage

This mission, tied to the nation's top-secret program, was now on fire, the black smoke calling attention to it in plain view of an emerging world-renowned city. The very next day planes and more people began to converge on the mountain to inquire. Dennis Schieck of the *Las Vegas Review-Journal* summarized the view of crews that flew over the site:

> *From the air it appeared that the fuselage from the wing's back is intact and there is a slight possibility that some passengers may have survived, although there was absolutely no sign of life anywhere around the plane. A complete veil of secrecy was clamped on information on the ground . . . all questions were countered with a grim shake of the head. The eight men in the rescue party boarded their special rescue lorry as the rising sun outlined peaks in the surrounding mountains.*

When the wreckage was first spotted on the afternoon of Thursday, November 17th, Mount Charleston was experiencing the worst weather conditions seen in years.

Aerial view of the crash scene.

Courtesy of Marcia Charter

Forest Service personnel gathered with military strategists and presented dire predictions for reaching the wreckage. Rangers said the snow was so deep, the wind so fierce, and temperatures so cold, rescuers would have to wait another seven months to get there. The military was not about to wait.

The sensitivity of the people and material related to this classified mission made Air Force Headquarters personnel determined to make it to the remote peak. The Air Force called on Colonel Pittman from Norton Air Force Base just east of San Bernardino, California and Colonel Schwikert of North Carolina.

"Concerning the classified material aboard, they impressed on me the necessity of speed in securing the area," Schwikert wrote in a letter thirty years later to a concerned group called the Silent Heroes of the Cold War. He recalled that his and Colonel Pittman's job was to ensure that top-secret documents and equipment would be recovered before the civilian rescue party approached the wreckage. First, they surveyed it from the air.

On that day (November 17th), I was the commander of the 42nd Air Rescue Squadron, based at March Air Force Base in California when we received the notice of the USAF C-54 on Mount Charleston. . . . It became our rescue mission. I dispatched one of our planes on the mission and went along myself. We over-flew the crash site and knew that no one survived. From that time on it was a recovery job.

The Air Force also deployed two parachute rescue teams with the hope of skydiving onto the site and offering first aid to anyone who might have survived. But wind conditions at the top of the mountain were so intense that the chances of the paratroopers hitting the mark were slim. That plan was abandoned.

The Air Force also tried to send a mountaineering team on foot to the wreckage in this hostile landscape that was entirely unfamiliar to them. Their plan was to use skis and snowshoes to climb the north face of the mountain and hopefully arrive in time to save any survivors. But from the base, the mountain terrain is deceiving. It is wrought with cliffs and deep pockets of valleys and trees. According to Colonel Pitman, it wasn't long before the team of snowshoers were climbing 80 to 90 percent inclines in waist deep snow. They had to stop and hunker down.

Team members recalled resting on a six-foot ledge, their sleeping bags dangling over the edge. Eventually, a few of the men reached the crash site and radioed the base camp: No survivors. They were ordered to go back and wait for a team with horses that was on its way. The members of the team spent nearly three days on the mountain. They made camp as best as they could about five miles from the crash site, using pine needles to keep warm in sub-zero temperatures.

All of this was going on away from the public eye. At the same time, Colonel Schwikert had realized he needed to reach out for help from the locals who really knew the mountain. He contacted Sheriff "Butch" Leypoldt of Las Vegas. Under Schwikert's orders, Leypoldt rounded up the Sheriff's Mounted Posse, a group Las Vegas volunteers who knew the mountain, but also knew about high altitude recovery missions.

Only a few years earlier, the Sheriff's Mounted Posse scaled the slopes of Mount Potosi a few miles northwest of Goodsprings to recover the body of Carole Lombard after a plane crash, as husband Clark Gable waited below. Unlike that mission, however, this would prove much more difficult and under a veil of secrecy.

Merle Frehner, one of the men in the posse, was about to have the worst day of his life, his daughter recalled. "It was awful I guess," she said.

> Butch (Sheriff Leypoldt) called and quickly told him the situation: They had tried for three days to get up to the plane. Leypoldt told him to get any people that he could. Butch particularly wanted Frehner's brother Vivian to come along because he had a snow-buster horse, because it had snowed (on the mountain) and frozen and snowed and frozen.

Vivian Brown's horse was named Joe-Snip. He was shorter and stouter than most horses, what you would call a "snow buster."

"Vivian didn't want to go but (he would go) if he (the sheriff) could get him out of work," Judy Frehner remembered. The sheriff got him out of work and in the tradition of the Sheriff's Search and Rescue team that still continues today, the volunteer team quickly responded to the call.

Pat McDowell was also among those posse members who would make the recovery attempt. McDowell clearly recalled the mission in a letter to the Silent Heroes of the Cold War. It wasn't clear to McDowell who was in charge, but whoever it was made it clear to him that they didn't want civilians participating.

The posse was assembled and ready to leave, when the Atomic Energy Commission changed its mind and refused to let us go, expressing doubt that we would ever make it.

After some convincing, Sheriff Leypoldt and the posse were given the go-ahead to strike out for the mountain. They set up a base camp at the Ranger Station in Kyle Canyon. Within a couple of hours, the two colonels, the sheriff, and the posse were getting ready. But neither the military nor members of the posse were very well prepared.

According to Colonel Schwikert, the military men didn't take any food or water with them, just several cans of Spam. Some members of the posse, on the other hand, stocked themselves with comfort food. McDowell recalls:

As we were preparing to leave, I had a pair of boot socks, one of which contained candy bars and sandwiches. The other sock contained a fifth of whiskey. I had tied the socks together and was about to put them across my saddle when one of the Colonels came up and asked what I was taking.

With a straight look on his face McDowell said, "snake bite medicine." McDowell was looking forward to the Colonel's reaction. "The man looked a little surprised and asked if I expected to run across any snakes. 'I might,' I replied. 'But if I don't, I've got a snake in the other sock.'"

Leypoldt also remembered in a letter that the day had started very early:

We were called in at 4:00 a.m. and set out from our homes, meeting at the Ranger Station above the Lodge. We set up a base there and unloaded and saddled up and were on the trail up the south face before daylight.

While it seemed to be an adventure at first, posse member Merle Frehner recalled to his daughter that they were quite unprepared for what was ahead. "We survived on one Spam sandwich and we even had to pay for 'em."

The team set out on snowshoes, avoiding the shorter and steeper north face trail. The route they took was longer to the top of the mountain, but it allowed them to bring along the seventeen horses, one horse for each of the passengers that was believed to be on the plane, and two additional horses to carry supplies.

Dewayne Brown remembered how his father-in-law said the shorter, stouter snow-buster horse Joe-Snip led the way.

"His head would move two feet to either side, and his neck would push the powdered snow aside so that they could get through it. Once in a while the sheriff's horse would break the snow, that's where it was three feet and not six feet. The first three miles was where most of the snow was."

As the leader on this mission, Sheriff Leypoldt carried a heavy burden. He had to strike a balance between the safety of his men and the military's dedication to guard the nation's secrets at any cost. He pondered this dichotomy while riding one of Frehner's horses, named "Firecracker," and climbing nearly 5,000 feet with this rough-and-tumble cigarette-smoking posse.

In no time at all, the drifts became so deep the horses' feet couldn't actually feel the trail. If Roy Naegle hadn't been along to guide us, I'm sure we'd have never reached the crash site. Roy was an old timer. He helped when the Civilian Conservation Corps built this trail in the early 30s and was probably the only man alive who knew the way up. We hadn't figured to be gone so long, so we hadn't taken any food. Man, there were times when the snow was so deep our feet would drag behind the saddle, so we'd get off and just hang onto the horses' tails and let them pull us along on our bellies. In those deep drifts, there was no other way.

It wasn't long before it was obvious that this mission wasn't for the weak. One of the posse members became severely ill and had to be carried down the mountain by three other posse members, according to McDowell. Frehner described the upward journey in his personal journal:

We started up the nine-mile zigzag trail. Gaining altitude, we ran into deep snow, three to four feet deep. Horses had to lunge to get through the snow. About one-third of the way up we ran into the snowshoe troops from March Field, encamped all in small pup tents. They had been there most of three days. They all looked half frozen. They invited us to have coffee, but we didn't have time to stop. We had another problem on top of the high ridge. Up there the snow was only about a foot deep. A cold north wind had frozen the top three inches into ice. When stepped on, a horse's hoof would break through the ice and cut his legs.

The horses' bleeding legs began to stain the crusty broken ice. By McDowell's account, the danger wasn't just the wind and snow, but the wounded animals themselves.

As we went higher, the wind increased in velocity and

blew the fine powdered snow in our faces making the
going still more difficult. The horses would slip and
fall off the narrow trail, pinning their riders beneath
them. Only the cushion of the snow saved them from
breaking their bones.

But the higher up the mountain, the less snow there
was, making the going easier. Seven hours later, at about
1:30 in the afternoon, and three days after the crash itself, they were finally nearing the crash site. This same
trail would have taken only half the time on foot in the
summer. The sight at this lonely wintry peak was surreal.
Sheriff Leypoldt remembered:

When we finally reached the top of this slope, there was
the plane. The nose and wings were on the down slope
and the fuselage just behind it, tail down. It looked like
it just snapped in two, like a matchstick. A couple of
Air Force officers told us to wait about 35 or 40 yards
behind while they went in first to check for classified
material.

The posse stood freezing with the mysterious sight in
front of them.

The ship had hit the mountain and disintegrated. The
pilot had evidently seen the mountain just before the
plane hit and tried to go over it, but failed. The plane
had pancaked on the side of the mountain. Cargo
and ten passengers had erupted through the top of
the cabin and everything was scattered 40 or 50 feet
in all directions. The motors were found 20 or 30 feet
from the plane.

The barren snow-covered peak was littered with debris and the charred fuselage looked like a broken me-
chanical whale. The half-frozen posse with their bleeding horses and body bags stood back and imagined what
could possibly be so secret inside that plane.

Whether it was because of their exhaustion or just an

illusion in the severe wind, altitude, and cold, McDowell and the other men's imaginations ran wild. From a distance, alone on that remote mountain top, away from the crash they thought they saw something very strange.

The oddest thing was the co-pilot. He was lying on his back some 30 feet ahead of the plane, buried in the snow. He was wearing flying shoes, which were all that was visible and those shoes looked to be a yard long. He looked like a giant from a fairy tale.

Meanwhile, the colonels rummaged through the crash site. Colonel Pittman examined personal effects as best he could on the frozen bodies in the blowing wind. One of the things he found was a watch with a shattered crystal. It had stopped at 8:19 a.m., possibly frozen at the time of impact. While the colonels were at ground zero of the wreckage, trying to make sense of their duty there, the posse members were getting restless, waiting. Posse member Merle Frehner wasn't about to be there slowly freezing any longer than necessary. He wrote in his personal journal:

Two Air Force colonels had ridden up with us, but behind us. They called a halt at the wrecked plane and rode the 100 yards up the peak. The freezing wind was blowing like 60 miles an hour. 'We are going to freeze up here if we don't get started going off this mountain, and so will our horses,' I said to the sheriff.

That was already on the sheriff's mind.

It was so damn cold, we could have frozen while waiting there.

The sheriff climbed up to the crash site where the colonels were fumbling around documenting the rubble around them, deciding if anything needed to be classified. Taking another look around and seeing that nothing obvious required isolation, the colonels gave their okay to start loading bodies on the horses.

In the thin air, the posse and its leader began another mission that would put their lives in danger. The mission was to preserve what dignity they could for these mysterious frozen dead men, men they had never known in life. The cold added urgency, as if death were swirling around them and they needed to do the job quickly in order to escape it.

Merle Frehner told his daughter what it was like when he and four others went to pick up the first body. Their muscles must have been drunk with adrenalin because the bodies seemed to weigh nothing at all to them.

We had forgot about dehydration and we almost hit ourselves in the face he was so light, like fried bacon. One by one they (the passengers) were found and put in body bags. With everyone picking up the wing I could see another body. I assumed the task of tying the bodies cross wise in the saddles.

Carrying the bodies through the snow and putting them in bags was one thing. Frehner's job of tying them onto the horses was not something he cared to write about in his journal. But it was something that Pat Mc-Dowell was brave enough to recall with sobering detail.

In order to transport the frozen bodies down, it was necessary to break them to conform to the saddles and to clear the narrow trail. It took three men to 'break' one body. It was a gruesome task and a blessing that we could not see what happened inside the (body) bag. It was impossible to break the pilot. Five men were unable to do the job.

The horses didn't like having the dead bodies cinched to their backs either, according to Colonel Schwikert: "I remember the horses were not happy with their job and needed some controlling to prevent their bucking." Some things are so difficult you never forget and this was one of them: "I'm 85 now and it all seemed like yesterday."

These men weren't entirely alone through this struggle; they were literally being watched from above. "All day long an amphibious plane flew around us with radio contact with the colonels," Frehner recalled in his journal. At one point Frehner says the posse sent a message to that plane. Since all the horses were going to be used to carry the bodies, it meant the men would have to walk down the mountain. So their message to the plane asked for more horses. That message went through the colonels to the plane, then to Nellis, and the response came back.

Knowing that we would have to walk out, because the bodies had to ride, we had the colonel's request that horses be brought up. But between the colonels, the plane and Nellis, the final message was, 'sending up hay.'

That kind of response would be funny under any other circumstances, but here it meant they were on their own.

By three o'clock in the afternoon, the men started leaving in groups of five, leading the horses on foot. The horses weren't the only ones who weren't happy. Leypoldt wrote:

Then we started down, figuring it would be easier than on the way up. It wasn't. Even though we didn't have to break trail, there was another problem. More than once, a horse would slip and roll down the slope, and we'd have to go down there and drag him back up onto the trail and start out again.

The path they had broken on the way up the mountain left chunks of snow that were now packed and frozen. "Walking down the mountain was like walking on boulders, all frozen solid," Frehner's journal reads.

McDowell and Leypoldt remember it the clearest, as the day began to turn the corner into night on the mountainside. The snow blew furiously across the treeless peak. They descended into the tall pines, the wind followed them, keeping it dark and blocking the view of the trail along the narrow ridges that marked their way. McDowell remembers that the altitude made it difficult for them to breathe and every step of the nine-mile trail was as slow as could be. At times, McDowell says they had to use shovels to clear the trail by hand before pushing on:

The trip down the mountain was a nightmare that I won't forget. The bodies extended over the sides of the horses, caught in the brush and trees, causing the horses to edge over on the narrow trail and lose their footing and fall. Dr. Clark's horse slipped and fell and rolled down the mountainside leaving the body on the trail. When his horse was once again on its feet and back on the trail, Dr. Clark found that he was too exhausted and weak to put the body back on the horse.

Darkness set in and the crew had no flashlights. Mc-

Dowell groped along the mountainside hoping that he would make it down alive, watching his companions stepping dangerously close to the edges.

Murdell Earl's horse was carrying the 200-pound pilot. He fell too, taking the body down the mountainside. By the time Earl had cut the body loose and dragged it back to the trail, he was unable to put it back on the horse, even with help. So another body was left by the trail to be picked up later. Ed Taylor, who had gotten off his horse to help Earl, who was unable to remount. We managed to get him back in the saddle and tied him on.

Still two miles from the base camp, all the men began to stagger and fall, holding onto the saddles of the horses for stability. At the base camp, four more sheriff's volunteers were being readied to back up the men who were floundering on the mountainside in the cold and dark. McDowell delved into his emergency kit.

I drank what was left of the snake bite medicine. It gave me a lift. I got hold of the horse's tail and let her pull me along but not for long. It suddenly seemed as though my guts had fallen out and I couldn't go another step. I said 'Cindy, I hate to do this to you, but you'll just have to carry double.' I managed to get on the horse, behind the body, and rode into the rescue station at 8:20 p.m. where I practically fell off the horse.

Twelve hours later and exhausted, Army doctors and ambulances tended to the men and fed the horses as they trickled in with the precious and secret cargo, which was quickly whisked away unnoticed. The last man stumbled in at midnight. Their path on the mountain was marked by a trail of blood from the horses' legs that were cut by the icy sheet they broke. Judy Brown recalled that her uncle's horse lost 100 pounds and many of the horses needed veterinary care after the ordeal.

The Sheriff's Mounted Posse members were clearly heroes, but the rewards were hardly reciprocal. After coming off the mountain, they were treated to steak dinners enjoying them like only half-starved, half-frozen men could after a 20-hour rescue mission at 11,000 feet. But at the end of their meal, the Air Force stuck each of them with a bill for the steak.

The Air Force's justification for treating the volunteers poorly was because, on the record, the whole mission never existed. Not only did they walk away receiving little gratitude for risking their lives, the volunteers were required to take an oath of secrecy. Only later that year did the Pentagon send a letter to the posse to commend them for their courage.

After the recovery, Merle Frehner went to visit his daughter and son-in-law. "Monday evening he and my

mother-in-law came over and he had the reddest face that I had ever seen him. They came in and sat down and he said, 'We went up on the mountain yesterday and got the bodies,' and he didn't have a lot to say because he was told not to talk about it. He said it was the most tired he had ever been in his life."

I had never ever seen him in a situation, the cowboy phrase 'calf roped.' I never ever saw him in a situation where he would give up.

There was a lot of speculation about how the accident happened and it wasn't helped by the colonels who shared their own speculation with the posse. The speculation was presented as fact.

"Merle mentioned one thing to me," Merle Frehner's daughter, Judy Brown recalled:

The wind was so strong that when they were trying to turn around to go back, that is when the plane crashed. The crash happened twenty minutes after they (the flight) would have normally landed. He said that he wasn't sure, but the plane might have gone as far as the edge of Utah and then turned back. The two colonels offered that information. No one else in the posse would have known that.

Like many of the families of the victims, Merle Frehner never knew the truth either. "He died in 1994 so he never did get to know what they know now," Brown said sadly. Over the years, "He didn't talk about it a lot," she said.

"There wasn't much to talk about. He did keep a couple of things from the accident," she said and read one of her favorite passages from his journal: "I still have the steering wheel. Any takers?" he wrote, as if begging to give it away and get rid of a difficult memory that he couldn't quite seem to let go.

Now the family keeps that yoke under close guard,

along with something that is literally morbid. "At the bottom of the mountain we still had fourteen body bags, but I think we got fifteen because we still have one," he wrote.

He gave that to his daughter, too. Forty-eight years after the fact, they found out who was meant for that fifteenth body bag. "There was one guy who slept in and missed the plane, and we have his body bag." It was a man we know now who, by his own account, never ever slept late a day in his life. He was never mentioned in the classified crash report, even though he would eventually rise to head up the private development of these top secret missions.

But these details weren't for publication. The extra body bag, yoke, and the colonel's story were the only artifacts these men had — artifacts that were small pieces of the story, overlooked in the following months, years, even decades.

As quickly as the spring sun melted away the bloody trail of the horses, frustration was felt by the families who sought answers. In an eerie premonition of what lay ahead, McDowell knew the truth of the wreckage would be picked apart and scattered across the world, possibly until it no longer existed.

The wreckage and shattered cargo is still on the mountain. Want a souvenir? Go up and help yourself.

The wreckage is now protected. Federal law designates it as a historical site. Taking items is illegal, though many have helped themselves to pieces of this history. But if the federal law and desecration of a historical site is not dissuasive enough, consider that visitors who take these relics may face a healthy dose of a fate similar to the Curse of King Tut's tomb. Something unwelcome follows the takers home.

CHAPTER III

Buried Secrets

Accidents don't happen on top secret military projects, or at least the military wants us to believe they don't. And if they do happen, they don't want us to know about them.

The saving grace is the efficiency with which investigators descended on the project from the first inkling that an accident had occurred to determine what went wrong. The Air Force cast a wide net over nearly everyone from within the airspace above to anyone below. They tried to collect the pieces of the puzzle of what went wrong, but left many of the pieces unconnected; after all, it was unlikely that anyone would ever scrutinize these circumstances, at least in their lifetime.

The classified report of the crash documents is the thorough work of two majors who collected official statements from control tower operators at three Air Force bases, from pilots who were flying at the time to witnesses at the tavern at the base of the peak. The final report is 157 pages long and is entirely unredacted. The pages are faded with the passing of every decade and today some are nearly illegible. Still, you don't have to read between the lines to figure out who investigators thought was to blame for the accident.

The pilot, according to the report, had simply become "disoriented." The blame seemed to be leveled squarely at the dead, as if they were victims of their own miscalculations. But the documents, as a whole now declassified and available, tell a different story.

Reading beyond the narrative, between the blurry lines, is evidence that specific rules weren't followed, from maintenance of the plane to flight forms, take-off times, and flight path orders. Protocols were ignored and the pages even expose a lack of written procedures for communication between air traffic control towers.

Investigators also missed or purposely omitted a crucial link. One would-be passenger was never even mentioned in the accident report, though he unknowingly played a key role in the plane's take-off time.

But back then there was a different attitude in the desert. Reading the report takes us back to a time when a Wild West attitude permeated these projects.

———

The report starts with a narrative that is not signed by either of the majors who investigated the crash. It begins with the matter-of-fact statement of how close the passengers were to avoiding a crash altogether. The site was just fifty feet below the crest of the mountain. The plane initially grazed the mountain and then the pilot steered the plane in a spiral to the left to try to stay airborne, but was only able to do so for another sixty feet before smashing into the mountain. There the wreckage and its victims slid another twenty feet, according to the report, before bursting into flames.

The wreckage itself was coldly dissected and documented by investigators, including where each part of the plane came to rest. When boiled down, the report is a sobering reality of a millisecond of violence. Three of the four engines were ripped from the wings. The propellers were torn from the engines. The engines were torn from the wings. The engines were hurtled through the air and where they rested, their heat steamed through the ice to the frozen rocks below.

Investigators took a look at pictures of the tachometers from two of the engines. They were frozen at 2450 rpm, the top-rated military speed for those engines, they said.

If the engines weren't operating correctly, that would be a clear start to assigning some blame. Maintenance records for USAF 9086 all seemed to be in order, but after poring over those mundane papers, investigators also found non-compliance with eleven technical orders. Those technical orders, according to the crash evaluation narrative, were not considered a contributing factor to the accident.

Since the plane itself wasn't to blame, investigators moved on to the people. This line of the investigation began with the victims themselves. Autopsies revealed everyone on board was killed instantly.

Each passenger was meticulously dissected. Their hearts, kidneys, livers, bladders, and all other organs were measured and weighed. The crushed skulls, lacerated bodies, and broken bones were all documented to the inch. Investigators concluded that during the accident the plane was reduced to large projectile sheets and spears of shrapnel that penetrated the victims' bodies. Some of the victims' bones were pulverized. Third-degree burns completely engulfed two of the passengers, CIA agents, possibly seated at the rear of the plane.

Modern forensic expert evaluation shows that the force of the collision tore nearly every organ in the victims' bodies from their normal positions and pushed them together into a grotesque mass. Nevada Senator and doctor, Ray Rawson also discovered an important detail that was overlooked in the report: Who was piloting the plane. The pilot would have been gripping the yoke at the time of the accident. Rawson concluded such a violent impact would have broken both of the pilot's thumbs as he gripped the plane's yoke on the path to their annihilation. George Manual Pappas Jr., according to the report, was found with both thumbs broken, indicating he was grasping the controls of the plane at the time of the crash.

Pilot qualifications

Pilot Pappas was a member of a crew that had been carefully selected for this secret mission. He was, by most measures, above average in proficiency. Investigators looked into the crew's flight records and found that instructors had described Pappas, Jr., as above average only three months earlier. The flight crew was considered "highly experienced" in the eyes of the investigators.

Pappas, the report said, had graduated from flight school in 1950 with 3,162 hours. His co-pilot, Paul Eugene Winham, had graduated in April that same year and had 682 hours, 409 hours in the C-54. His flight evaluations by instructors showed "satisfactory" performance.

But their handling of technical details of their flights is puzzling. According to the investigation, almost none of the pre-flight forms were filled out correctly, despite the pilots' experience, from fuel to weight, even to the number of passengers. These details were a red herring to a bigger problem that doomed the flight: weather reports. Other pilots who had taken this same route to

Watertown told investigators that they had never been given weather reports for their actual destination at the secret airbase. They were only given reports for Las Vegas. Investigators found that Pappas, like all the other pilots, was never even briefed by telephone about the weather, as was required by Air Force protocol.

Investigators couldn't determine at what time the flight actually left the airport, but they did determine it was between 7:00 and 7:25 a.m. If Pappas had gathered a weather report, it may have occurred at the time the flight path was called in at 6:13 a.m. By 7:25 his weather reports, if he had any at all, would have been more than an hour old. A storm can go a long way in an hour.

For some reason, investigators didn't look at the weather reports from 6:13 a.m. that morning or even 7:25 a.m., but they did review weather reports near the time of the accident and found that an extreme weather front was headed toward Nellis Air Force Base.

This weather front, they wrote, included openings in the clouds that looked like passages to clear sky, also called "sucker holes." At about the time of the accident, the sucker holes were rapidly changing, opening holes in the clouds on the east side of the mountain where the C-54 and Pappas would have been trying to navigate by visual means.

The classified investigation report simply speculated that after the pilot cancelled his use of instruments, he tried to descend through one of these sucker holes but was engulfed in clouds, the mountains all around, hidden. According to the investigators, the pilot simply became disoriented. While that may be true, it is an oversimplification of an entire package of miscalculations that led Bissell's Narrow Gauge Airline into a death trap.

The flight path

Interviews with personnel at the Watertown Command destination revealed that pilots' previous orders on this path were to fly along the east side of the Spring Mountains over the busy airspace of Las Vegas. Las Vegas was a maze of air business and the top-secret flight through this area would seem a contradiction. But it was in that sea of air traffic around Las Vegas that the pilots would normally cancel their use of instruments and fly by visual means to the north. That original plan worked and was safe. This route and instrument navigation cancellation through Las Vegas, at its least, included a weather station.

With the desert's typical clear skies and still dry air, a weather station might seem unimportant to casual visitors to the area. Anyone who has been here for a year, however, has seen violent storms that form somewhere out there in the barren wasteland and suddenly approach the Las Vegas Valley without warning, catching even the weather service off guard. A weather station is critical on a daily basis, no matter how calm and clear the skies seem.

USAF 9068, and supervision of its path, was determined by investigators to be under the control of the Commander at the Watertown Airstrip. Only a security officer at the Atomic Energy Commission was authorized to establish a destination in the event of bad weather. That security officer's role in the flight path was never explored by investigators. Instead, investigators turned their attention to technicalities, literally gripped to the purpose of finding fault with who was at the immediate helm of the doomed craft.

Typically it is at the yoke of a plane where pilots call for 'visual' flight status. They do it at a pre-determined point called "The Let Down." According to the documents, the Air Force rules require that the Let Down have a weather station. And they require it for good reason: Flying without instruments, the pilot may not know if a storm is coming or might cross his path.

So where on this flight's path was the required Let Down point?

The classified investigation three days after the accident showed that Captain Francis Kane, another pilot who often flew out of Burbank to Area 51, had permanently filled out Pappas' flight plan with the words: "Weather checked by pilot," indicating it would be the pilot's responsibility to check weather, but he wouldn't have to record the findings. The investigation also discovered that the tiny town of Goodsprings, Nevada was inexplicably used as the point of instrument termination or the Let Down.

Goodsprings, Nevada, is about 40 miles south of Las Vegas. Today it has an automated weather station, but 1955 was before automation; a weather station would have had to include a human airport weather observer, who would have relayed information to pilots like how high the clouds were, the layers of clouds, the visibility, and any obstruction like smoke or clouds, anything falling from the sky and storms, wind speed gusts and direction. That information would have been priceless to Pappas on that day in 1955.

This location as the Let Down was a new mix in the path of flights to Watertown. According to the report, this was only the eighteenth time the crew had flown this route. With flights twice a day, which was the typical pattern between the bases, the first flight on this new path would have been only nine days before the accident.

When investigators started to look into this new flight path, they found that a 'route flight check' was never performed on it as required by Air Force protocol. They also found that for some reason two flight plans were recorded. Investigators found that pilots told them that the dual system eliminated the need to file even a clearance from Burbank.

As investigators looked into it further, they found that the problems with the new route were clear to one man from the start. This man was on this new flight path on the very day before the accident, according to the investigation.

Major Reid Carney was interviewed the day after the crash. He was the officer on the project responsible for writing the "Standard Operating Procedure" for the crew on this flight. He personally flew with any crew on their first flight to the secret airbase. His mission was to "ensure familiarization with the route," he told investigators.

According to the report, Major Carney was on the new route to Watertown for the first time in the C-54 on November 16 with Pappas as the pilot. Major Carney told investigators that out of curiosity, he decided to ask the pilot about this new route, even though he was supposed to be the one in charge of familiarization with the flight paths. The pilot told him that the new route established the town of Goodsprings, Nevada to terminate the instrument navigation instead of the Las Vegas range station as had been previously used, because it saved about ten minutes of flying time. But he said Pappas also said the new procedure was to ask Nellis Air Force Base for weather conditions after they had taken off. It's not clear if that was ever done and no one interviewed at Nellis said that it was done. If it was done, was Pappas ordered to make the flight anyway that day regardless of the weather? We will never know.

Major Carney told investigators he "intended to try to have the route change cancelled as soon as he could contact the necessary personnel," but he didn't say why. Was the route too dangerous? Was the Let Down with no weather station a problem? Either way, the message that the flight path should be cancelled somehow didn't make it to Pappas even though Major Carney was speaking to Pappas directly. Investigators didn't even ask why Major Carney didn't cancel that flight path immediately with Pappas. If he had cancelled it, the fourteen crew members would still be alive.

Investigators continued on with their interviews. On November 30th, in an interview with Captain Francis Kane, Air Force investigator Major Greathouse apparently stumbled across the origin of the new flight path. Captain Kane was a regular pilot on these missions. He told Greathouse it was a good flight plan and he would use it, he said, as long as there were "visual" flight conditions:

> Major Greathouse: *Who was the, or as far as you know, what person changed that route?*
>
> Captain Kane: *I believe Lt. Pappas was the one who wanted that on account of the jets flying over the Las Vegas area there.*

But Kane went on to tell investigators he didn't know where the directive came from.

The highly experienced Pappas was already dead by the time investigators were looking to lay the blame. Carney and Kane appeared to have the last words, words that laid blame squarely on the shoulders of the deceased pilot.

Communication and records

The investigators' last mission was to explore what went wrong with communication, if anything. Groom Lake, also known as Watertown, was on the map of *probable* flight paths on page 70 of the report. But according to the report, the flight was *destined* for another location: Desert Rock Air Force Base, near Indian Springs, Nevada, which was one of three air bases that Pappas would have tried to contact.

Pappas had returned to using his instruments because of the heavy snow showers, according to the Military Air Transport Service out of Kelly Air Force Base in San Antonio, Texas. Almost as a tribute to the importance of weather reports, the classified documents stated that it was too late for Watertown to transmit the weather conditions to Pappas, because there was poor radio communication and by the time the storm had reached Watertown, Pappas and his doomed passengers were already in the throes of the storm.

Investigators concluded that Watertown didn't contact the right agency when the aircraft first went missing. Remarkably, the right airbase wasn't contacted because there "was not an established procedure at the Watertown Airport governing the control of aircraft." Watertown should have contacted other agencies that had jurisdiction over the flight, the classified report said. While Watertown struggled with its isolation and lack of procedures to deal with such a case, clouds had quickly begun to thicken around the plane destined for the clandestine desert base.

> It seems probable that the pilot on encountering lowering visibility and ceiling turned to the left to fly away from the higher terrain, which caused the aircraft to be flown into higher mountains. It is also probable that the ceiling and visibility was even lower in the immediate visibility of the higher mountains.

The report says it is probable that the flight was blown "to the east of the mountain range (on the Las Vegas side) that was unknown to the pilot." Pappas turned westward to avoid higher mountains, which would have forced him straight toward the even higher cloaked mountains; with lower visibility, he flew directly into the storm with strong winds blowing down on the C-54. How strong? Those winds, "could exceed the climb capabilities of the C-54," investigators wrote. The setting that was found on the wing flaps of that plane was set at 10 degrees. That setting would not be used, investigators said, except as a last resort to clear an obstacle.

Clearing an obstacle is undoubtedly one of a pilot's essential skills. Investigators concluded the most probable cause of the accident was pilot navigational error, trying to fly through mountainous terrain by visual means when instruments were needed.

The importance of instrument use was obvious on other flights in the area that survived that day, according to the investigators' interviews. Pilot Edward Okerlund was among those who made a prepared statement for investigators. He was flying at 6:00 a.m. from Nellis to Indian Springs and conditions were already incompatible:

In flying this course and returning to Nellis AFB, we were forced to remain below an overcast whose bottom was at 7,000 feet.

During a break in the weather when he was flying back at about 6:45 in the morning, the clouds were already very close to the peak of Mount Charleston itself. Another pilot, John Carmichael, told investigators he couldn't even recall being able to see the peak of Mount Charleston as he was flying that day.

Since it was so clear to everyone in the air that day that flying conditions required instruments, it raised a question: Why was USAF 9068 even flying, especially when investigators found written flight orders from Watertown that clearly stated all flights in and out of Watertown would be conducted under visual conditions only? The answer is easy: a complete lack of communication of weather reports. Again, was Pappas ordered to make the flight despite the weather? The project security officer was on board and he had complete jurisdiction over the flights.

When it's all said and done, the flight departure time for the C-54 wasn't relayed to Watertown until 7:47 a.m. By that time the pilot had already cancelled the plane's use of instruments. At 8:40 a.m., the Watertown operations officer called Nellis to ask if anyone had heard from the flight. It wasn't until ten minutes later, a full thirty-one minutes after the men were already dead and their bodies freezing on the mountainside that Watertown called again to authorize the flight to land at Nellis because of the bad weather.

The report calls an attempt by Watertown to divert the aircraft to Nellis "questionable." There was no established procedure for the control of aircraft, it says, and instead of contacting other air bases, Watertown should have called the March AFB Flight Service Center.

A memo from the President of the Board of the Military Air Transport Service recommended that better coordination be maintained between control towers and that their communication stations obtain the correct time of take-offs.

Investigators dismissed that point, attributing more weight to supervisory error in establishing Goodsprings, Nevada as a point for terminating instrument flight because it had no weather station. They also said flight-time errors contributed to the accident, but even if the pilot had gotten a weather briefing, the procedure would have proved inadequate.

Flight time errors, however, seemed to lead to an overall chaotic picture of the communication and time between the three air bases as they tried to locate their lost flight.

Major James Voyles, who was at Watertown at the time of the accident, was interviewed by investigators and tried to recall what happened that morning.

At 7:30 a.m., he got a call from Burbank that Pappas had left at 7:25 a.m. But thereafter, investigation documents paint a portrait of desperation at various control towers.

Staff Sergeant Alfred Arneho, who was interviewed by investigators on November 23 and heard the C-54 pilot's high-frequency transmission, told investigators that after the heavy traffic had cleared at his airbase, he asked another operator, presumably at Watertown, about the flight. That operator was presumably Major Voyles, who told Arneho the C-54 was overdue at its destination. So Arneho said he made a blanket call to it. "In the blind sir," Arneho recalled of his call on every channel to the C-54 at about 8:30 a.m., but there was no answer.

Voyles confirmed that at 8:30 a.m. he called Nellis to talk about weather there. Ten minutes later Voyles said he called Nellis again to ask if the C-54 had been heard from. But it wasn't for another thirty minutes, at 9:08 a.m., that Voyles called March Flight Services to ask about position reports for the C-54.

At 10:15 a.m. he finally made the difficult call to March Flight Services to report that USAF 9068 was overdue, almost an hour and a half after the flight was expected and he should have made the call. Voyles told investigators he kept trying to make radio contact by using both the "B" and "D" channels.

By that time investigators found another sergeant, Hillman, who was also at Watertown. Hillman told investigators that he remembered calling Base Operations in Salt Lake City. The last record they had of USAF 9068 was cancelling IFR (instrument flight restrictions) over Goodsprings at 8:08 a.m., he told them. Eleven minutes later, they were dead. Hillman said he called every airport from Cedar City, Utah, to McCarran International Airport in Las Vegas to ask if the flight had landed there.

It wasn't until 3:40 p.m. that an A20 spotted the wreckage. Nellis dispatched a helicopter, but it had to return because the wind was too severe. Colonel Mixon of Watertown and Captain Ryland of Air Rescue arrived just after 5 p.m. and took charge. The rescue mission began with another troop of unsung heroes.

Where the investigation ends is where the mundane detail of flight times becomes important.

Investigators wrote that flight-time discrepancies contributed to the accident, but the question is how could such a detail contribute? What seems like a minor detail may be the most telling clue to the overall atmosphere that doomed USAF 9068. For some reason the departure time and discussion of it is exactly what's missing from the report. Either investigators overlooked it, or they purposefully left it out. No one really knows when the flight left, and that calls into question how long that window of opportunity was for them to get a weather report or alternative instructions.

What *is* included in the investigation is that USAF 9068's last report to air traffic controllers was to Burbank Airport at 7:12 a.m. at 9,100 feet. But even that is disputable. According to the proposed flight plan that was supposedly filed by telephone that morning at 6:13 a.m., the time of departure was to be 7:00 a.m. The actual time of departure listed on the Air Force forms in the crash report was 7:25 a.m., based on the message that was sent to March Flight Service Center that morning from Burbank.

The details of why Pappas left late were never explained by investigators. It turns out Pappas had once promised a crew member that he would always wait for him. As we now know, that passenger never showed up and by the time Pappas decided not to wait any longer, his weather reports, if he had them at all, would have been nearly an hour old.

The implications of that, combined with another statement in the report, are clear. "The error in transmission of the actual departure time of the aircraft resulted in a delay in the attempts at diversion by the operations personnel at Watertown Strip," the report says.

The death of the passengers on this doomed flight sheds light on the disastrous effect of secrecy over safety — that if no one knows what is happening, no one can ensure that protocol is being followed. The painful truth is that this was the nature of the project that some say made it successful, yet also jeopardized lives. While the report characterizes a key element in the crash to be the flight path and that it was Pappas' own maverick choice, cutting corners wherever possible to achieve the mission as efficiently as possible was the one unwritten protocol over all procedures at the time.

Making changes

The deadly results of the Air Force's obviously uninspected procedures, if nothing else, led to a culture to ensure the safety of future flights. In the days following the horrendous accident, safety took precedence over time and secrecy. Weekday flight departures were changed to 8:00 a.m. every day except Mondays and return flights were scheduled for later in the day and for good reason: For the pilots.

Captain Kane: *Better rest, also, we continue on into Las Vegas and cancel our IFR (Instrument Flight Restrictions) there and proceed on to our destination on VFR (Visual Flight Restrictions). Also we check in with Nellis tower to ensure a 10,000 feet ceiling in order to proceed on in.*

Major Greathouse: *Have any other weather requirements been changed?*

Captain Kane: *We have to make a personal weather check here at Burbank, which I've always done anyway.*

In addition to ensuring adequate weather reports and take-off times, the investigators recommended five points, all quite obvious, including identifying an appropriate place for being cleared to use visual flight status and procedures to ensure adequate control of the aircraft operating into the Watertown airstrip. Who would ever ensure that these recommendations were followed? It was, after all, secret.

Silencing the evidence

Someone did try to acquire all these embarassing crash details from the military only a year after the accident. This inquiry inspired a stern internal warning for military eyes only. A partial text of the memo is inserted in the pages of the classified crash file that includes the disturbing directive.

The memo was written by Colonel Dorsey, the Director of Flight Safety Research for the Air Force, dated January 1956. The colonel states that on January 4th, a "Mr. Defek" came to his office requesting information about the accident. Mr. Defek, according to the memo, said that his company was involved through an "indemnity policy" because civilians had been killed in the accident. Colonel Dorsey says he told "Mr. Defek" that the report of the accident investigation "was not available."

After Mr. Defek left, the request set off alarm bells. Colonel Dorsey went on to write the memo outlining a directive that could effectively shield original reports like this. He called for "Collateral Investigations," or, in other words, as he put it, investigations that could be conducted by other agencies.

It is in our interest that such investigations be conducted whenever it reasonably appears that litigation and claims against the Government involving large sums of money are likely. Collateral investigations may eventually be our only real protection against a Courts' subpoenaing our accident investigation reports.

Colonel Dorsey went on to say that the practice of "collateral investigations" was a routine practice until it was discontinued in 1955. The memo explained that the Office of the USAF Judge Advocate General and the Tax and Litigation Office both continued to advocate these reports. The directive in the memo was to "remind" military investigators that they could recommend "collateral investigations."

The memo implied that a "collateral report" was a kind of shadow report — one that might omit some key internal investigative information.

It's not clear if such a collateral investigation was conducted in this instance, but if so, it was not included in the declassified U-2 documents of USAF 9068. One family did successfully sue the government for large sums of money, and Colonel Dorsey's memo was specifically geared toward these high profile and high dollar lawsuits.

If there is any question about the government's intent to cover up the crash, just look for the record of it in the Military Aircraft Registry. According to the registry, C-54 USAF 9068, Serial #44-9068, Douglas MC-54M-DO, Construction # (C/N) 27294 was listed as continuing to fly missions for decades after the crash. On record, it was simply withdrawn from use (WFU) in 1970, fifteen years after it smashed into the side of Mount Charleston, killing everyone on board.

For the military's purposes the mystery was solved. The government moved on, cleaning up in its own way, leaving a big mess behind both on the mountain and for the families of the victims to deal with for decades.

According to the front page of the classified document that has a list of people who requested and read the document, only three people ever looked at it. The names are illegible.

The classified report is an interesting mish-mash of material. Inside is also a letter addressed to the Air Force from the Forest Service. The letter stated that the area where the plane had crashed was federal land under the jurisdiction of the Forest Service, and half of the body of the plane remained there on the peak. According to the classified file, Forest Supervisor L.A. Dremolski wrote to the Air Force concerned that hundreds of hikers might "prowl around the remains of the plane's fuselage with the possibility of it slipping over the steep cliff with some of them still in it."

Dremoliski made a suggestion that he said was relayed to him by one of his rangers: "The wrecked fuselage could be shoved over the cliff into the canyon below, where it would no longer be a hazard to the public." But it was just a suggestion.

I am just passing this on for your information and am wondering if you do make any disposal of such wreckage and if you have any plans for this particular situation.

If the military didn't have plans to dispose of the wreckage, it certainly would develop some now. With the backing of the Forest Service, the military sent explosives to attach to the gutted shell.

The Air Force contacted a demolition crew of four men from Nellis and Lake Mead that included Herbert E. Dobberstein, a 33-year-old Chief Gunners Mate with bomb disposal expertise at the Lake Mead Armed Forces Special Weapons Base in 1956.

The details of this demolition would have been lost to history, too. But decades later, Mr. Dobberstein happened to see a newspaper article one day about the Cold War collection being developed at the Atomic Testing Museum in Las Vegas. The articles reminded him of some photos he hadn't looked at in at least "fifty years," he told museum staff. He brought them to the museum and, though he knew little of what they represented, let alone that they were tied to this still classified project, he gave them to museum curator Vanya Scott. Despite the fact that there wasn't much evidence that this was an important mission, she wanted to hear his story and took detailed notes.

Mr. Dobberstein recalled that in a briefing room with the Air Force about this demolition, his team was shown pictures of the crash. To avoid suspicion, he was told that the plane was headed to the Nevada Test Site from Los Alamos, the other atomic testing ground when it crashed. The Forest Service wanted the plane carried away "but AF had no transport helicopters able to take away the pieces. The Air Force and Forest Service agreed to reduce the size by explosion."

The Air Force did make an effort to "salvage the four engines, which were new at the time." The engines were taken down by teams of horses, but neither that detail nor the fate of the engines is mentioned in the crash investigation, which had already been long closed and sealed.

The photos the Air Force shared with the demolition team were supposedly taken in the spring after the crash as part of the orientation to the mission. But some of those photos clearly showed members of the posse with body bags loaded on the horses — a detail that wasn't shared with Dobberstein and he wouldn't have known what was in those bags on the horses. But he kept those photos which are now pieces of the puzzle of history.

In September 1957, Dobberstein climbed to the top of the mountain and rigged the fuselage with TNT and C2. At that altitude, the explosive plume quickly ballooned into the sky and was gone within seconds, as if none of it were ever there at all. Dobberstein has since passed away, never knowing how these pieces of history he had held onto for so long would come back together.

Explosion sequence of USAF 9068 taken by demolition team, Spring, 1956. The plane's turbines were removed by an Air Force helicopter.

Courtesy of the Atomic Testing Museum

The explosion burst the fuselage into thousands of pieces, scattering them down the mountainside, thousands of feet into a valley below. The final resting place for some of these parts ended up at the lowest point in the valley near the base of the mountain, in an area called Mary Jane Falls. It's a place that is both ravaged by avalanches in the winter and in the summer is loved by families who marvel at its trickling showers of water from the cliff's towering walls. Most visitors would have no way of ever putting these tiny bits of history strewn around them back together into something meaningful. But forty-nine years later, a family camping at Mary Jane Falls was visited by something unexpected: a sounding board to the prison of silence for the victims, victims that couldn't and wouldn't be ignored.

CHAPTER IV

Lost History Discovered

Hundreds of Boy Scouts have climbed Mount Charleston since 1955. Most have seen the wreckage, but that's all they knew: Plane wreck, no date, no mission, no death toll. Just the remnants of a hardly recognizable plane crash.

In 1972, seventeen years after the accident, one of those Boy Scouts was 12-year-old Steve Ririe. As he climbed the mountain, the scoutmaster fed Ririe's curious mind to help push the young man up the seemingly endless switchbacks to the top.

"My scoutmaster mentioned that there was a plane crash and it captured my imagination," Ririe, now in his 40s remembered.

I wondered what it would look like. We were exhausted by the time we made it there, but not too exhausted to rummage through the wreckage. I had a friend, Pat Compton, and he came up to me and said, 'Look, I found a dead man's belt buckle.' And I thought that was so neat. When you are twelve years old, you don't have the maturity to understand death. I just thought it was kind of neat.

Ririe didn't find anything so 'neat' there, but he came down the mountain with a couple of pieces of aluminum from the wreckage in his Levi pocket. He squirreled them away.

You know as a kid you have a little junk drawer and I rummaged through it one day and I had those little pieces of aluminum in there for many years.

Thinking back now, he realizes that was the beginning of something that would consume a great deal of his life. Over the years he would come across those little pieces of aluminum in the junk drawer and would think back to the moments high up there on the mountain.

It was kind of interesting; it stirred my imagination. I remember sitting at the crash site and wondering what happened? I asked the scoutmaster what happened and he said he didn't know.

Eventually Steve became a scout master himself, and it became his job to pass on his curiosity of the mystery behind the crash. He would sometimes casually talk about it to the young men and other people who climbed the mountain. "I would say to them: 'I went up there and I wish I knew what happened at that plane crash.'"

I know people who have lived in this town for many, many years and no one ever knew. No one even remembered what had happened.

Steve's voice became a unique beacon in a world of silence about the crash. So few people talked about it; in fact, one of the most remarkable clues to what happened in the accident was right next door his entire life and he never knew it. His neighbors, the Browns, were relatives of one of the posse members.

I never asked them. I didn't know that they knew anything about it. Everyone I asked didn't know anything about it.

But even if he did know they were involved, they didn't have much more information than he did. Over the years talking to people, Ririe was often disappointed. It seemed the only people who wanted to talk about this mystery were those in a culture of conspiracy theories who had concocted stories of their own.

There are a lot of people that think they know every-thing about it but they don't know anything. They will tell you crazy stories about the plane being lost and circling over the dunes of Utah before trying to go back to California.

Steve didn't buy that. He wanted facts. "It became a kind of mystery for me. It wasn't a pressing issue. I was just kind of curious."

Asking around about it seemed to be a lost cause. The collective memory of the incident seemed to have been forgotten, overshadowed by the city of sin, scattered across the far reaches of the nation and world by its transient population. Over time, as hikers carried away pieces of the crash site for keepsakes, they carried away memories that would be no more than filler in some junk drawer far away, eventually also dismissed, unknowingly helping to serve the military's purpose of ensuring secrecy by hiding it piece by piece.

By 1998, Steve was going through tough times, marital trouble. "When you are going through personal trials, it is part of our nature to escape and make some sense of your life." His escape, he decided, would be to return to a happier time in his life. That happy time was when he was 12 years old at the Mount Charleston crash site. Seeing the crash site would be 'neat' again, he said, but his real goal was to climb to the top of the mountain, a kind of personal accomplishment.

He called some old friends to see if they wanted to

come with him. One said he would go with him, but backed out at the last minute. So on a Saturday morning in September he drove up the mountain at sunrise alone. Normally, the mountain would be teeming with people hiking to the top at that time of year, but not on this weekend. It seemed deserted.

It felt like I was up there alone. I ran across two people. When I was first starting out this guy came charging up behind me who said he climbed the mountain once a week.

That man was long gone by the time Steve made it up all the switchbacks to the meadow hours later. Another hiker going down the mountain passed him.

He didn't even look up at me. He just looked down at the ground. I was glad though because I was kind of in a contemplative place on my own. I thought it was unusual though.

Steve kept going up the mountain slowly and alone, and when not far from the crash site, he thought back to when he was a child and wondered how much of the plane wreckage would still be there. As he got closer, it was obvious that the place had changed dramatically from what he remembered seventeen years ago.

When I got up there and looked at the crash and had the understanding of an adult, I just kind of sat down next to the propeller. I just looked at the contorted propeller and how it was twisted and realized right then that whoever was on this plane did not survive.

Steve pulled his eyes away from the wreckage, turned around, and looked at the mountain ridge, realizing the few feet it would have taken to clear this final obstacle in the middle of open air as far as the eye can see. Sitting near the rubble, he stared at it. The cold wind curled through the twisted metal and wires.

"The wind was blowing over the ridge, just really blow-

ing." That's when something a little strange happened.

As I sat there, I laid back and closed my eyes and let the wind rush over me and I got this feeling like I was not alone. It was so creepy that I kept looking around up and down the trail thinking 'who in the world . . . is there someone up here?'

He closed his eyes and tried to imagine the plane. "And what I saw was this big silver plane with a big tail and an oval door flapping in the wind. It was the weirdest strangest thought. It just felt like I was not alone."

After a little while there, he shook off the feeling and hiked the rest of the way to the top. His main goal was to sign his name in the register for hikers who had summitted the mountain. Once he reached it, he unceremoniously scribbled his name and slipped the book back into the plastic bag, leaving it there for future visitors.

It doesn't take much for Steve to remember exactly what it felt like as he began to leave.

I started back down and the temperature is kind of cool. When you get up there and you can see the lake, all of Las Vegas, Pahrump, the Sierra Nevadas. The

The only recognizable remains of USAF 9068 were the twisted propellers that sat unmarked for decades as visitors passed by.

Courtesy of Silent Heroes of the Cold War Corporation

ridges of mountains in the distance are purple. I re-
member it being so incredibly beautiful. I didn't want
to leave. It just really made me feel good.

He hiked down through the meadow that was sprin-
kled with violet, yellow, and white flowers. He didn't
see another person the entire way back and didn't think
another thought about the plane crash until two or three
weeks later, about three o'clock in the morning. "I woke
up and my thought is the plane crash."

At this point, Steve really had no proof that anyone
had died there, just a sneaky suspicion. A sense of urgency came over him. "I thought someone ought to do
something for these people, find out who they are and
put up a plaque."

It was a nice thought and that's all it really was, a
nice thought. Steve went back to sleep. But sometimes
a thought becomes a passion and passion is not far from
obsession. Little did he know, it wasn't the last time he
would wake up with the same thought.

Morning after morning after morning, I would wake
up at the same time and think about this plane crash.
'That dawg gawn plane crash.' I don't remember a sin-
gle dream, but I must have been dreaming about it.

Steve says he would lie awake for 20 or 30 minutes
early every morning without being able to sleep, and
these thoughts would tumble over and over in his head.

It really started to get to be a weird thing and I didn't
want to tell people, including my wife because she would
think I was a little bit off my rocker. So I started asking
people, *I really started digging.*

As nonchalantly as possible, with a line of questioning
specifically designed to appear to be casual conversation,
Steve asked everyone he came across: How long have
you been in Las Vegas? Oh, by the way, have you ever
heard anything about that darn plane crash up there on

Mount Charleston?

Steve seemed to hit a dead end with everyone and the obsession only got worse. "It was very few nights that I got a full night's sleep."

After eight months of waking up every morning at the same time, with the same haunting thought, and asking every person he happened across, he remembers one day driving along some street in Las Vegas. It was as if thinking about the plane crash was strapped to his head with duct tape, occluding his view of the road ahead.

I remember pulling off to the side of the road and saying to myself out loud, 'I have gone as far as I can and so whoever you are, unless you give me something, it's over. Let me get some sleep.'

It wasn't long after that he got his first break. Steve was at a fundraising event for the Boy Scouts and met a man who was selling a book about the history of Mount Charleston. The author was Richard Taylor and he had a son named Russ. "Russ and I grew up together," Steve said with surprise, discovering that throughout his life, he was remarkably close to people who could lead him to the story. Steve called up Richard and they talked a little bit about it. Taylor only had a small section about the crash in his book: that it was rumored the people on board worked for Lockheed, that they were working on the U-2, and that they were on their way to Area 51.

So then I started contacting everyone, the Air Force, Nellis, trying to figure out if anyone knew anything about the crash and it was really hard to do.

It seemed Steve had hit another wall as solid as the mountain itself. About this time, with marital troubles behind him, he and his wife decided to take a camping trip with their two daughters. They decided on Mount Charleston and specifically Mary Jane Falls, directly below the crash site. His wife was still oblivious to the obsession that was eating her husband alive. They started up the wide gravel trail to Mary Jane Falls and into the trees. But where the trail started to turn and head north up the steep canyon to the falls, the family left the trail and went up the valley toward Mount Charleston directly under the crash site.

We took our dog Fluffy. I had in my mind that it would be neat to be close to the plane crash because it had been in my thoughts for so long.

Steve, his wife Julie, and their two daughters were the only ones there, because hardly anyone ever camped at Mary Jane Falls, let alone left the trail to where Steve and his family were camping. They pitched their tent, made their dinner, and went to sleep. His wife, Julie, thought she was in for her usual pleasant sleep, this time in the quiet solitude of the mountain. She says she always sleeps deeply, so she never knew Steve was waking up at night in their bed back home in the valley below.

But this time it was her turn. "I was sleeping, and I woke up scared," She said. "I never do that. I sleep like a rock. My dog had snuggled up next to me and it wasn't really cold and I was thinking 'What is Fluffy doing?' and 'What is wrong with him?' Because he never does that."

Julie didn't know Steve was awake too, but he heard their little dog whimpering. Julie decided to go back to sleep.

I said, 'Ok, something must be wrong with me.' I went back to sleep, but I woke up again with a start, the same way!

Julie had the strange feeling someone was lurking around their tent, so she sat up in the dark and silence with only that thin wall of nylon between her and the dark forest outside, wondering if anyone was out there.

I kind of thought to myself, I have never believed in Big

*Foot or in aliens and it was a weird feeling. I looked
out of the tent and there was nothing. Steve was kind
of stirring.*

Again she put her head back down and closed her
eyes.

*I had this dream. I saw this guy in a captain's hat. It
looked like a 40s or 50s old outfit; it was kind of a
brown Air Force like thing. His hat had a round thing
on the front of it with a band around it. I saw him
trying to talk to people.*

She laughed nervously when she recounted all of
this.

*I just saw him trying to get people's attention and no
one could hear him or see him and he was frustrated
and sad. And when I woke up again I knew he was
there.*

Her first thought was "I never want to sleep here
again. This is scary, I don't understand this. I was sitting there and I listened to Steve to see if he seemed to
be awake."

Honey, are you awake?

Yeah.

I can't sleep, can you?

No, I can't.

*Are you a little freaked out? Because I feel freaked
out.*

Steve said he felt the same way. Out of the blue, she
blatantly asked him, "Who is the guy in the captain's
hat?" hoping that he would know something about the
same strange dreams. To her surprise, Steve immediately
sat straight up and looked at her and said, "What?"

It was time for Steve to tell Julie the whole story. He
started by asking her if she knew about the plane crash
in 1955. She said she did, but no real details. He told
her the plane crash site was right above where they had

pitched their tent. He didn't know that parts of the plane were scattered all over the area around them, that their tent was in the midst of its graveyard.

Julie remembered their late night conversation. "He said, 'I just keep waking up at night and feeling like they are there,' and I just said 'okay.'" Everything Steve said was making her a little nervous, but she didn't show it.

But Steve didn't know anything about the "man in the captain's hat" that Julie had seen in her dream. She told him about the dream. "Well, he is here right now, and I can feel it." She told Steve, 'You had better find out what he (the guy in the captain's hat) wants.'"

I said that when we were in the tent. I had the feeling that something was pressing on the mind of him (the man in the captains' hat), that he was upset that there was something undone. When I asked Steve if the man with the captain's hat is here for you? Steve said 'I don't know, I think so.' And I said that 'you should find out. Obviously there is something here.'"

Neither of the Riries have ever believed in ghosts and Julie was extremely reluctant to tell this story. "If I hadn't had that dream I wouldn't have understood (what Steve was going through), and I would have been less sup-portive of Steve in this," Julie said. "It became personal to me, too. I respect him for it."

That's how she feels now, but for the next two years it was a very trying time as Steve openly pursued his obsession, no longer having to hide it from the family. Little did they know, a similar experience to the camping trip would eventually follow the entire family home and do more than just keep Steve awake at night.

I would kind of lose interest (in finding the answer to the crash) and I wouldn't be working on it as hard anymore and then suddenly I would start waking up at night again.

It wouldn't leave him alone.

After that second trip to the top of the mountain when all of this began, and after a year-and-a-half of trying to live a normal life, Steve made his way to another Boy Scout picnic. There he ran into a man named Bob Drabrant, a civilian who worked at Nellis. Steve sheepishly mentioned, as he always did when he met anyone, that he was interested in what happened at the crash site. "I was very, very cautious when I talked to people because I didn't want them to think I was off my rocker, because if they asked why I wanted to know, what would I say? Oh, just curious."

Drabrant was really receptive to Steve's questions and told Steve he should call Lockheed because the company was operating flights between the atomic test site and Burbank at the time. A few calls to Lockheed and a receptionists put him in touch with public relations person Gary Grigg. "When I first started talking to him," Steve recalled about asking about the crash way back in the 50s on top of a remote mountain top that everyone in the world seemed to have forgotten about, "he (Grigg) was apprehensive and said 'this is kind of a strange request.'" Gary told Steve that he would do what he could. There were a couple of old guys around Lockheed and Gary said the best he could do would be to ask them. But he also told Steve to check with the CIA because the CIA was Lockheed's customer at the time.

Steve wasted no time calling up the CIA. Making his way through phone systems, eventually a CIA employee named Onya was on the other end of the line with him. He remembers telling her:

I am looking to see if I can find the history of this plane crash. She said, 'we get a lot of people calling about UFOs' and she said, 'here's the deal, everything to do with the U-2 was declassified in September 1998.'

This was the big break for Steve. His insides were exploding with enthusiasm. Of course Onya didn't know it. "Yeah, she said, they had some conference or something." She was referring to a big ceremony commemorating the U-2 project and its participants. That ceremony happened to be the same month and year that Steve took his trip alone to the top of Mount Charleston and had the feeling that he wasn't alone.

Steve recalled:

It was the fact that I discovered the U-2 was declassified the same month and year I was on the mountain that completely freaked me out. With everything that was happening it really helped confirm to me that the weirdness I was experiencing wasn't my imagination. For all I know, I was on the mountain the same week or day the U-2 was declassified. I didn't learn about the ceremony for several years until we found the Marr family. There were so few families actually contacted by the CIA that when the Marr family told me about the ceremony I was very disappointed.

All the documents associated with the U-2 were sent to Maxwell Air Force Base and were available, according to Onya.

Of course, that was Steve's next call. He remembers his conversation with someone at Maxwell AFB in some sort of records collection office. "A guy named Archie said to me right off the bat: 'You aren't going to find any UFOs and you aren't going to find any little gray people.'"

Steve laughed and said he wasn't looking for any of that, just trying to find out something about a plane crash at Mount Charleston a long, long time ago and the people who died there. Archie told Steve he would need a couple of weeks; it wasn't going to happen overnight. There were tens of thousands of unfamiliar files.

It looked like Steve's frantic run of phone calls was dying. Two weeks was a long time for Steve.

I am still being woken up at 2:30 most mornings and it got real crazy with that right about then and I kept thinking this has got to be the end of this. I was thinking that he (Archie) is going to come back in two weeks.

To Steve's relief, Archie called just three days later. Archie had the report of the mysterious plane crash that had haunted Steve and kept him awake at night. To Steve, that report was priceless, but for just $14.00, Archie said he would send it to him overnight. Steve had it sent to his work so that he would know as soon as it arrived. When it was hand-delivered, Steve dropped everything and left work. "I then went right to the library and got on the microfiche and there it was. I am staring at the names of the men that died in that plane crash!" He wasn't really sure what to make of those names tucked in the 157 pages of cold, hard facts in jumbled narratives of investigations, pictures, and autopsies. Steve felt that something very powerful was still missing, but he didn't know what it was.

A few days later Gary Grigg from Lockheed called Steve back and said, "There is a guy here who knows some of the guys that were on that plane. He said what is even better is that one of the children of the people who perished on that plane works for us now."

When he spoke to Bryan Kreimendahl from Lockheed, the son of a man who died on that plane, it became apparent that Steve would have some serious footwork on this path laid out before him.

Bryan was very interested in Steve's accident report. Bryan was so young at the time of the accident that he knew very little about his father's work and nothing about the other people on the plane nearly fifty years ago. Steve was breaking new ground and developing a picture of history, a picture he could try to piece together from bits of the torn images. In exchange, he might get some sleep and a sense that he had done the right thing. But talking to Bryan was more than just a piece of the puzzle on this long path; it started to uncover Bryan's personal life and the pain associated with the loss of his father. Bryan had to be willing to open up to Steve, this stranger who appeared out of nowhere and apparently had the answers Bryan had been looking for his whole life. Bryan offered the first personal story of coping with the accident that Steve had heard.

It was such an amazing experience to talk to him. This is something that happened to me. I never set out to do this, none of it. Honestly it happened to me. I can't even describe in detail how I was being pushed by this force and I know it sounds kooky and at first it scares the crap out of me.

After the conversation with Bryan, Steve still had more than 13 families still out there somewhere waiting for the same awkward conversation. Steve bravely started to contact them one by one. Steve wasn't really sure what he was doing. Was he really searching for more answers or was he just the bearer of a cruel truth and cold accident report?

In between trying to contact the families, Steve thought back to his original thoughts on the mountain in September 1998, that someone should do something for the families of the crash victims. He began to contact the media. He gave an exclusive interview to chief investigative reporter George Knapp at KLAS TV, Las Vegas Channel 8. This renowned journalist's story about Steve's discovery led to a mushroom of interest from citizens, and a little help. Steve was contacted by media outlets across the country, which he used to try to get the word out: This Boy Scout leader out in Vegas has an accident report from 1955 and wants to find the families of the victims.

——◆——

"I came home from California on January 21 and the first paper I read was January 22, 2001," Las Vegas resident Marian Kennedy recalled, reading about some stranger whose professional life included writing insurance policies for AAA, who had somehow stumbled upon a significant accident report. "I was reading about Steve. And I was getting phone call after phone call since I had come home from vacation, but I kept picking up that article until I finished reading it."

As Marian Kennedy read the article about the crash, one of the names seemed to ring a bell. In 1998, the same year Steve made his return to the mountain, Marian had been researching her genealogy and found the US Census pages from 1900 when her great-grandparents lived in Covina, California.

"My grandparents had orange groves, maybe fifty acres. Silent (a crash victim), his parents had an orange grove. I was on the census, looking on the census pages, the 1900 census pages. I have a film, an old, old film.

"Here is Harold Silent (one of the victims) at age four years old, and it bonded me. Four land parcels over." The project suddenly had a new and vested meaning to her, too, like it was one of her long lost relatives.

The hair stood up on the back of my head. I was just dumbfounded that my parents probably knew Harold Silent when he was a young lad. They had social functions they did back in those days. I thought, Hey, he (Steve) is going to need some help finding the families. That would be terrible for them to hear something on the news like: 'I had a brother or father that died up there.' I thought they should know before they ever heard the news. So I called Steve up at his office. I told

*him I would stay with it until I found everyone on
that plane.*

He would take any help he could get and so she set
out for three months on her own mission, contacting li-
braries looking for obituaries, flying to gravesites around
the nation, and calling numbers in phone books.

"It was a real roundabout way, but that's the way I had
to do everything. You just keep trying to get people to
help you," she said. She wasn't a librarian, but she knew
that in each community she called, librarians would be
a strong ally in the search for information. She said
without question, they took her calls and the information and ran with it.

As she found the families one by one, she would call
them. "You had to go easy with it, we are not dredging
up anything. I said, 'all of this has been released now
(public information).' They were very anxious, very, very
anxious." She said that they had burning issues. "Some
hated the government; this had happened during peace-
time; 'why did he die on a mountain top in Nevada?'"
they asked.

Hate is a strong word, but that's the impression Marian got when she made first contact with some of the
families. Over time hate may have been replaced with
understanding, the kind of understanding Marian and
the Silent Heroes of the Cold War were hoping to bring.
Today, Steve feels strongly that most of the family members have grown to be intensely patriotic, even though
the families believed that the government was somehow
to blame.

This mission was not only one of discovery, but one of
healing, and both Steve and Marian had their own need
of internal discovery and healing. It brought meaning
to their lives. Marian coped by feeling compassion for
these families. "I must have been brought in psychologi-

cally." She said, "I put myself in the shoes of the families." Steve and Marian both knew they could never truly understand. Steve said,

I would like to say that I understand the depth of the suffering that these people went through all of these years. It came as a huge surprise to me that it would bring up all the sadness, not having closure and this would complicate and add to their suffering.

Steve and Marian shared the duties of researching and calling the family members, knowing that every call might bring a gush of emotion.

As Steve made these phone calls, his habit of waking up at night seemed to stop entirely, but it was replaced with a new question that caused him suffering: "Lots of times I wondered if I was doing the right thing," he said. Steve assumed that the families would be grateful for finally learning the truth, regardless of the fact that a call out of the blue would rehash some of the worst memories of their lives, but some of the families didn't want to have anything to do with him.

I started to realize that those families, some were still living under this shadow of a clandestine operation that had been covered up in their lives.

The phone would ring somewhere in America. An unsuspecting person would answer, not knowing what was about to be delivered from the stranger on the other end:

My name is Steve Ririe and I live in Las Vegas and I am just interested to know if you are related to 'so and so' that perished in the crash on Mount Charleston in 1955.

"In every case there was this kind of silence," he said, and in that silence he would eventually hear a weak, apprehensive voice say one word: *Yes.*

One of these families was the O'Donnells. First they

wanted to know who the hell this insurance employee, Steve, was and why he had the truth they had long been searching for. They didn't want just a name, they wanted proof. Steve got the help of a police officer to verify his identity for them, so that they wouldn't think he was part of some kind of hoax.

It (his calling them) was way too weird for them. You start hearing some of these stories and in opening up there was this pain and sorrow that they have. Growing up without a father, their mother could never tell them.

Over the months of getting hold of the families, he found that some wanted someone to blame for all their suffering. He had to treat them with "kid gloves." Some blamed the government; others blamed the pilots. Steve suddenly had to become the unofficial defender of the pilots, explaining to the families that both pilots had logged many hours in the C-54 and both were qualified to be flying.

Steve Ririe was coming out of the blue with news the families had long ago resigned would never come. Digging up the accident report and tracking down the families literally had opened a can of worms. Decades of questions that had festered deep inside were finally being resolved, like who was at the yoke when the plane crashed.

The call Steve made to the co-pilot's brother led to an instant moment of healing. "It was a big relief (knowing that his brother Paul wasn't at the controls)," Troy Winham recalled when he read the report. "Knowing that he (Paul) was a top notch pilot and the possibility that he had made a mistake was always a question in my mind and so it was a relief to know he wasn't at the controls."

A network of families across the nation began to grow. Passionate e-mails between them and Steve had people at computers at both ends of the national communication lines in tears. For some, the unanswered questions that grew over time became sources of deep confusion and conspiracy. Larry Hruda, for instance, wrote to the Silent Heroes of the Cold War:

> *Thanks to you, I now have the strength to start pursuing this more for all of the families. I can't take back that time. I have no idea where to start but I really feel that the CIA needs to do all the work on this one. They have the resources.*[3]

Hruda began to sift through old paperwork. "I found many documents with my father's signature on them. After laying them all out so I could look at them all at the same time, I believe that some are not his."

> *This all started me thinking about the whole cover up and once again I started wondering about what the real truth is so I had to stop.*[4]

A month later, the same questions still remained for Larry.

> *I wish some CIA big shot would come to my house and say 'Son, I am agent whatever and I am here to tell you the truth about your father, what he did and what he gave to his country.*[5]

Many of the families had simply given up long, long ago. Richard Hruda's daughter, Joy Cunniff told Steve.

> *I don't think I would have gone looking myself. I have picked up a little bit of information since you started this thing, but I really don't know very much. No. I tried to question my aunts but they don't know anything because they were so young at the time. And everybody else that I know is dead.*

Later Steve asked her how she felt now that her father might be memorialized as a hero. "I felt very strange. It felt unusual. I don't know how else to say it, and it felt very weird."

It felt weird because family members seemed to accept the loss and accept their suffering in private. Something was holding them back. There were a few who took a proactive approach, trying to find out something like Larry Hruda. Even those who tried to uncover the truth needed someone like Steve to come along at the right time. Larry wrote to Steve:

I feel that there is a reason behind everything and there is a reason that you were chosen for this task. Maybe it is because the rest of us are in too much pain to deal with it all. I tried (to get answers) for a while. I called and called and got nowhere. Sadly the hurt took over and it was affecting my job and my life so I had to stop. I learned long ago that I cannot change the world no matter how much I try. This is true of my search for my father. I tried time and time again to find him. I called the CIA about four years ago and asked for their help, but all I got were empty promises and a big phone bill.

Steve came up with one interesting and somewhat complicated plan to help bring closure to the families. He organized a trip to the mountain for them. In 2001, they embarked on a journey that Steve had once done alone, looking for the answers and people that were now with him three years later.

Bryan Kreimendahl was among those at the lodge at the base of the mountain where visitors had witnessed the accident. He fulfilled his own long-standing natural curiosity when he met with the other families there.

When I quizzed the family members as to their knowledge of (their relative's) involvement with the U-2 project, they told me they didn't know anything at all until Steve Ririe notified them just a few months ago. I felt so bad for them. I asked Fred's wife, who was married just seven weeks before her husband's death. I asked if she was notified at the declassification of the U-2 project and the subsequent CIA ceremony in 1998 about Fred's involvement with the U-2 and the answer was no. I cannot understand how our government could not locate Mrs. Hanks or any of Fred's immediate family. So here we have what appears to me to be a very close family of genuine Americans that have no knowledge of their older brother's contributions to a project that was critical for our nation's security.[6]

While driving home from meeting the other victims and sharing their common questions, Bryan thought about how the crash had changed all their lives.

I also had the sense that we, the family members of the victims were all related, perhaps not by blood but certainly by events. . . I don't know what force struck Steve Ririe or what motivates his group of volunteers but in my mind, these individuals are performing a great service for which our government has shown little interest. Steve and his volunteers are also members of this related family and I thank them very much for their efforts.[7]

Bryan Kreimendahl also recalled of his father:

We have been FORCED to think about what this has all meant. After my father's death he was always represented to us as "perfect." I know this can not possibly be true, but for lack of any better information, that is the way I know him. When I think of these fourteen individuals losing their lives in their prime and what they could have accomplished in their lives, it saddens me . . . I have never felt so much emotion so many times in forty-six years as I have in the last six months.[8]

Also among the hikers that day was Joy Cunniff. She went along with the hope of recovering some understanding of why she had lost those birthdays and Christmases with her father.

"It was very difficult. No one knew what happened. We didn't talk about it a lot," She remembered while resting on the rocky trail.

What I miss most now is the relationship like the one between my husband and my daughter.

But the higher she climbed the mountain, the more nauseated she became from the thin air, and she stopped two-and-a-half miles short of the site that changed her life.

"I think she was getting closer to something that was tangible, yet not tangible. She has a lot of stuff to work through," Larry Peterson, one of Hruda's cousins said.

Cunniff's daughter, twenty-seven-year-old Brenda Cummings, also made it to the crash site on that hike; though she never knew her grandfather, just being there was overwhelming and she began to cry.

"It's incredibly emotional," she said. "I don't know whether it's the wreckage or what happened here. I just wish she (Cunniff) could see it."[9]

Julie Ririe remembers it as a continuation and culmination of a spiritual rise as she walked through the meadows.

When we hiked up there with the families, I kind of had the same feeling (camping at Mary Jane Falls). We were walking through there. I was walking with Keith Rogers (reporter) and Joy Cunniff (relative of crash victim) started getting sick. Keith sat down with her. Steve came back. She (Joy) said, 'you guys go up.' When we were sitting there I felt like they (the ghosts of the victims) were there.

Julie didn't say anything at the time, because she says it felt like a personal moment and didn't want to disturb Joy. Later Joy did open up, telling some people there that she had felt especially close to her father then.

It was extremely difficult for just about everyone who was thrust into the situation, including Julie Ririe: "I haven't talked to anyone about any of these things to anybody but Steve. I don't want anyone to think we are kooks."

But Steve had no choice; he had to explain why he was pursuing this, and along the way tried to fumble his way through something he felt he had no control over.

"It was kind of something external, like someone or something was trying to get something through to me." As he continued pushing on, there was a sense of relief.

Yeah, absolutely a huge relief. It was more the frustration of it. It was a feeling that I had to do something next, a proverbial door to go through somewhere but not knowing where it was.

As a result of opening these wounds, some felt the release of a decade of anxiety, but it literally killed one mother. "When all this surfaced, my mother had a stroke and it affected her mentally and we were overwhelmed with the care she had to have," the sister of James "Billy" Brown recalled. The night of Ririe's climb to the crash site with the families, the Brown family sat at the bedside of James "Billy" Brown's mother. Ririe recalled what the family told him happened that day:

She turned to her children and said in a weak voice: 'Now they'll know that Billy was a hero, won't they?'

'Yes, Mother, they will,' one child consoled. She died that night.

One thing Steve says he did that was a mistake was sending some of families full copies of the accident report. It was too graphic, including autopsies of their loved ones' bodies, bodies so mangled that they were sealed in caskets by the CIA. The report's one saving grace was that it proved the victims died instantly, with no pain.

"Honestly, I found reading the report very interesting," Bryan Kreimendahl said, whose comments filled an emptiness in Steve's own life by filling a long-standing emptiness in the lives of all the victims' families.

It answered a lot of questions that I never had answers for, exactly what happened, what went down, the horseback riders, the recovery teams going up on the mountain.

Steve said family members told him they were going through the same emotions he was, only more intense. Family members would say to him, "I never knew any of that story until you started bringing this up and I found it very, very interesting; I found it very, very interesting."

Steve also found it interesting, because it never occurred to him that the crash might have been kept secret and the details kept from the families. Steve's efforts had grown from being his own secret mission only to grass-roots support from families and finally full circle to the government itself. Former Nevada State Senator Ray Rawson called him and said he had been going to the crash site for years and felt something was there. Rawson himself took up the cause, pushing the state and eventually Congress to pass legislation to turn the site into a national memorial. With sixty-two sponsors and co-sponsors, the final resolution of the Nevada Legislature was enacted.

Resolved, That the Nevada Legislature hereby urges Congress to declare the crash site of United States Air Force 9068 near the summit of Mount Charleston as the "Silent Heroes of the Cold War National Monument"; and be it further

Resolved, That the Secretary of the Senate prepare and transmit a copy of this resolution to the Vice President of the United States as the presiding officer of the Senate, the Speaker of the House of Representatives . . .

Part of accomplishing the goal of creating a national memorial meant one last trip to the top of the mountain for Steve to bring down a relic that could be publicly displayed, something that visitors to the base of the mountain could touch, even if they couldn't touch the crash site itself. Steve's new mission was to dismantle the very artifact that once made him realize men had died there on the barren mountainside—the twisted propeller. That propeller would be the centerpiece in the memorial. On May 8, 2002, a dozen men and a helicopter were back on the mountain taking it apart. Once they had brought it back into the valley, Steve put the propeller parts in his garage at home.

That opened up a whole new chapter of weirdness.

It affected his wife more than him and it happened not long after that last journey:

I was the only one home; they (Steve and the kids) had just left the house. I heard some footsteps walking up the stairs and toward the bedroom. I said, 'I thought you guys left.' The footsteps were that loud. But no one answered. Right then, all the hairs on my body stood up. 'Who is in the house?' I thought I was going to get killed. I thought there was an intruder in the house. I said, 'I am leaving this house.'

Then Julie says the family noticed that the door between the garage and their house seemed to open all the time on its own and when it opened, no one was there. Once Julie even heard the lock or the handle turn.

This kept happening over and over. One time I was walking in the garage and the door opened toward me. I had that same feeling; I am going to get killed (thinking it was a home invasion). I don't understand this, there is no one there. Then I started relaxing. It's not alive, whatever it is.

She said to herself, "There is no one here."

After she started to get used to these unusual events, Julie's little daughter said something to her out of the blue one day that really creeped her out.

My daughter said that there are people going out into the garage and looking at the propeller. I said, 'Honey, are you seeing people with your eyes?' And she said 'no, I just know.' Then I said to Steve, 'We need to get the plane parts out of the garage. It is scaring everyone in the family.' So I made him take it to the storage unit and we haven't had any problems since.

That's where the propeller has been since 2002, in a storage unit, locked away in the dark, waiting for a permanent home, where you and I, and the spirits of the men who died, can be free to visit them.

Demolition team members take a break on the way up Mount Charleston.

This photograph of the wreckage taken from below the ridge by the demolition team on the south loop trail shows how close the plane was to clearing the mountain.

The long flat ridge below the accident site shows the direction of approach of the sheriff's posse. The lack of snow at the ridge shows how hard the wind would have been blowing at the time of the accident.

The plane's nose was unrecognizable.

The aluminum shell of the plane is crumpled like paper in this view. In the background a member of the sheriff's posse is seen leading a horse carrying a body bag.

Close-up view of the emblems on the C-54. A crushed tail wing on the right indicates the right-hand side of the plane (uphill side) suffered more of an impact than the left.

Interior view of fuselage shows where passengers would have sat.

View of the wreckage from the ridge above documented by the Air Force shortly after the accident. If the pilot had reached the point of perspective of the photographer, the plane would have cleared the ridge.

This propeller was torn from the engine itself and buried deep in the earth far from the wreckage. The twisted propellers were the only recognizable remains of the crash site by 1998. When Steve Ririe saw the propellers, he suspected no one on the plane survived. One of the propellers was later disassembled to be included as part of a national memorial.

One of the wings of the C-54 was virtually untouched. The tremendous force of the impact tore the engines away from the wings. The engines were later recovered by the Air Force as a cost saving measure.

The fuselage was so unstable according to the Forest Service that it could be rocked back and forth. The rear hatch door was also loose. This would be the same door that Steve Ririe saw in his daydream.

A gauge, books, and other personal items strewn about after the wreckage. One Boy Scout who later visited the site said he found a belt buckle.

Gauges provided clues in the accident investigation indicating the maximum engine speed of the plane at time of impact.

Measuring the extreme angle of the wings and trim at the time of impact showed the emergency measures taken by the pilot in the flight's final moments.

Radio frequency device that would have been critical to communications between flight crew and air traffic controllers.

Demolition team rigs wreckage with explosives.

CHAPTER V

Silent Heroes
of the Cold War

The following stories by friends and family of these deceased heroes are short, disjointed accounts and memories of the lives of remarkable men. Men whose lives were cut short, leaving large gaps in family histories. Their stories present a picture not only of American life in the 50s, but their work that led to the end of the Cold War. Few of the families knew what happened to these men or their role in helping to end the war. Though they suddenly disappeared, and their families suffered in the name of national security, their legacy now lives on.

Courtesy of Bray family

James F. Bray

Occupation:	Security, Previously OSS
Employer:	CIA
DOB:	January 29, 1907
Age:	48
Marital status:	Single

I must admit, I cried the first time I saw my Uncle Jim's name on the list of victims. I also realize now that I never finished the grieving process after his death in 1955. I was 14 at the time. I didn't really know how to deal with it. Uncle Jim was my boyhood hero, Michael Bray wrote to the Silent Heroes of the Cold War.[10]

As testimony to how close this family was, Michael's father was also named James, as if the two brothers were inseparable, at least by name. But they led very different lives, like only the family of a CIA agent could know.

James F. Bray's life began like any other. A student and football player at Notre Dame, he graduated with the hope of becoming a teacher. Later he joined the Kansas City Police Department. When WWII broke out, he enlisted in the Army and became part of an intelligence detail. He landed in Normandy around June 6th and it was his job to search for German informants.

At the beginning of the Cold War, James was back on American soil, planning to live behind his own version of the Iron Curtain on a 20-acre plot of land next to his brother's family in Texas. People who passed by would never know that James was even there. Behind his brother's home, James had built what looked like a shed. But it was a fortress, made of blocks with a steel roof and garage doors. His nephew, Michael Bray, helped him build it.

We was there one day carrying something or other and his knee went out on him from that old football injury and he fell down and was writhing in pain and he said to me, 'What you have to do Mike is yank it and pull it straight out.' I thought, 'that was kinda weird.' But I did it and he was fine. We picked back up what we were carrying and went on.

A tough guy indeed: One who lived in that little block shed with the steel roof and garage doors. In the back of the shed, away from the view of the street was a screened-in area where he could sit out of sight. Inside the dark windowless building was a tiny kitchen, a tiny work area, and tiny bathroom. His niece used to help clean the little dwelling.

He had a place there that he lived in, but by looking at it you wouldn't ever know anyone lived there. He didn't have a telephone. We [the family in the main house] had a telephone and if we got a call for him we had to buzz him.

Dolores Bray-Koza remembered. She was only twelve at the time of the accident, but she would never forget her kind uncle who lived out back.

I remember his face and I always knew he did something really secretive. He would leave and told my dad 'I will tell you where I am sometime.' So as I am older I realized how incognito he lived. He was a very generous man but never married. His work was what he did.

But when he was home, he was a family man. Michael recalled:

My brothers and sisters and I adored him. Whenever he was in town, we would play games at the dinner

*table. He had an invisible friend that was under a
napkin. We rode into town with him to get the mail
and he would take you to the five and dime and get
you something and so I guess you could say he spoiled
us. He was in some ways like a brother.*

"My brother would always ride with Uncle Jim and he
was a family man without having his own family." Dolores said. "He (Jim) and my father had great dreams of
what they wanted to do on their land there."

*They had a dream of having a farm and a ranch,
and had purchased land together, 20 acres, and dad
was 10 years away from retirement. They were getting
ready for retirement together and would have run this
cattle ranch outside of Houston. And that never happened,* recalled Michael.

James kept these dreams and family insulated from
his stressful work, but Dolores knew whatever he did
was tough and it took its toll.

*He had an ulcer and whenever he was home he always
ate with us and my mother prepared special meals for
him knowing about his ulcer.*

As part of the job, he would just disappear sometimes.
And then one day out of nowhere came the news that
would shatter their life-long dreams. Dolores saw the
men come to their door.

*I remember the day he died like it was yesterday. I
remember the two men, how solemn and somber they
were and my dad knew instantly that something tragic
had happened. I think they [the CIA] went out and
cleaned out my uncle's house before they even told
my father.*

She says it hit her father the hardest.

*It was like a month or two where my dad was im-
mobile. Back then you just didn't talk about things.
Communication back then wasn't like it is today with*

families.

A few days after the accident, a letter came in the mail from James. Michael still has it.

It said, 'I am in L.A. I have a dental appointment and will return to the [Air Force] base Thursday morning at 8:00 a.m.' That was the day he died. We got that letter in the mail 2 or 3 days after the crash. He had mailed it from L.A. In all the years that my mom and dad knew Jim was working with the government, my mom told me that they would get letters from him that he would return next month or whatever. But, the only time he was ever explicit about the time he would re-turn was the day he died.

Their father tried to cope with the loss by taking a trip out to Mount Charleston the following year. Dolores remembers riding horses to the peak.

The following summer we went to Las Vegas. I remem-ber how grief-stricken he was, and how long it took us to go up to that mountain. We went by horseback and rode up to the top of that mountain and there was a lot of debris at the top of that mountain. There was still a lot of stuff, even personal stuff. He [father] did bring some stuff down. It was a whole-day ordeal. It was a very frightening trip. It was just rock, the trail wasn't very wide.

After two hours of rummaging through the wreckage, she says her father didn't come back with much. One of the relics he carried down was a pot that was used to serve hot coffee to passengers on the doomed flight, possibly to his brother.

The suffering continued for the rest of the family for decades.

"As a kid, he was one of my real heroes." Michael re-membered. "For six months or a year I would have a re-curring dream I would find out that he didn't really die."

While the difficulty lasted six months for Michael, his father never really recovered. "You could just tell," he said.

No, he wasn't the kind of person who would share his emotions. I realize now that this was one of the major tragedies in his life and he never really recovered from it. There was a piece of his heart that was gone.

It wasn't until forty-five years later that the Silent Heroes of the Cold War contacted what was left of the family to tell them what Jim was doing when he died.

"Kind of proud of him, to tell you the truth," Michael said when he learned about his uncle's association with the U-2 project.

He finally met other families, too.

I met some of the younger CIA agents who were working with my uncle. One told me the story about when they were finished building the thing [U-2]. One of them said, 'Hell they didn't even get [the U-2] to the end of the runway [at Area 51] and the thing took off'. It was so well made. It was an amazing machine. It was a camera with a plane built around it.

He learned that his uncle was the chief of security on those routine flights to the secret airbase.

Dolores says her uncle was generous, but they never truly understood how generous he was until his death. By never marrying, he spared what could have been even more family members the pain of dealing with the mystery of his death for so many decades. Dolores knows other families weren't so lucky.

If they lived not knowing, I can't imagine. And I think that is why my uncle never did marry was because of his job. He was very intelligent, very nice looking, very well educated.

Michael says you have to take the secrecy of the time in context. The fact that the flight was ordered to proceed without radio communication was the fatal ingredient in this flight. It was also a necessary precaution, he says, to prevent the enemy from learning the location of the super secret spy plane.

Today, you say that they were paranoid, but when you think back to 1955, Russia, atom bomb, hydrogen bombs. I can remember as a kid atom bomb drills. I remember my older brother saying that if he had a negative about the whole thing, is that the pilot that they had wasn't the most experienced pilot. But the pilot didn't want to die that day; it was a tragic accident.

The Brays were never notified of the declassification of the crash documents or invited to the U-2 declassification ceremony in Washington. The Brays were the second-to-last family to be found by volunteers of the Silent Heroes of the Cold War in 2000, two years after the accident documents were declassified. That is also the same year James Bray's mother died. She never knew her son's role in the U-2 project, but Dolores said her grandmother did remember her son as a generous hero in her own way: The son who always took care of her.

Courtesy of Brown family

James William "Billy" Brown

Occupation: Security
Employer: CIA
DOB: August 25, 1932
Age: 23
Marital status: Single

Unlike many of the other families who got word of the accident, Billy Brown's family didn't hear about it through the television, even though Barbra Brown-Wolling, Billy's sister, remembers that she was 11 years old, watching the news with her family at the time they learned of the accident. *The night we got that call, my mother and I were watching television and the phone call said: 'Operator 5 calling James Brown.' It wasn't long after my father's birthday. When Daddy came home he made the call.*

There had been an accident, that's all the operator said. Now at age 63, Barbra still remembers what she imagined would happen next upon learning Billy had been in an accident: "I can picture us going into the hospital and seeing Bill with his leg in a cast."

But that's not what they were in store for at all.

My daddy was hysterical. We had neighbors and friends who came over. And we went for days . . . it seemed like an eternity, wondering whether or not they had reached the crash site.

Details about the accident trickled into the family, details about the fact that there was a storm and the flight was without communication through unfamiliar mountains on a new route.

I was upset at the way I found out the way the plane was flown and I can remember my daddy to this day asking the men in the CIA: 'What in the world was so important that you had to send a plane out in that kind of weather?' he said.

But their family understood this world of secrets better than many of the families, because Barbra's uncle was also a CIA man. He was the one who flew out to Las Vegas and identified the body. She remembers that he accompanied Billy's remains back to Savannah and "he marked the casket. He got out his pocket knife and put an X or something."

The mere fact that someone in the family had seen the body provided a little consolation that other families of the victims didn't have.

Well, I don't think we were as misled as some of the families were. We knew it was a top-secret type thing. And that's what came to be.

While that's what came to be, they never stopped wondering. Forty-five years later, Steve Ririe, who never knew Billy Brown, found out the whole scope of what Brown was involved in and made that call to the family as he did with all the others, out of the blue. "My, what a difference a day can make . . . little did I know when I woke up on March 23, 2001, that this day would forever change my life."[11]

Sam Wolling, James Brown's nephew, recalled the day he heard the truth and it brought back all the memories of his uncle.

"Uncle Billy," as they called him, was his "grandfather's best friend, my great-grandfather's hunting buddy, my mother's idol and my grandmother's pride and joy," Wolling recalled.

Billy Brown was destined to live a life of service. He had a strong commitment to charitable organiza-

tions. He was an Eagle Scout and loved the outdoors. He could always be found on some sort of fishing or camping trip.

His experience as a Boy Scout had kept some of the family members' hopes alive, that he was somehow still alive on that dark remote mountain in the days following the accident.

We were certain all the survival skills he learned while on those trips with my great-grandfather would help sustain him if stranded on top of Mount Charleston. Only later did we find out there was no chance of survival.

How many times I have wondered how my life would have been affected had I had the chance to truly know my uncle.

As hope faded over the years and the questions took a seat in the back of their minds, Wolling said he always suspected his uncle was a hero.

He graduated from the Georgia Military College and was accepted into the University of Georgia. He was admired by his friends and teachers and elected an officer in his fraternity. He had a magnetic personality. And that drew him to the CIA.

As I look back on Billy's short life, I marvel at all he was able to accomplish. He was good to the very core of his soul, a young man who desperately loved his close-knit family and who sacrificed his life for the freedom and well-being of his countrymen.

Barbra Brown-Wolling recalled her favorite memories of him: "I adored Billy, I worshiped him. He wasn't home a lot. He was home holidays and he went off to school at the Georgia military college."

When he was home, it was pure pleasure.

He would always go get a deck of Old Maids and that was the highlight of the visit home with me, to play

Old Maids with me. He was very, very friendly, always smiling . . . tall and thin. He had a date one time to go down to the beach and I wanted to tag along and I did and when we got there I said I wanted to go into the water and he said I will go with you when I count to 1,000 and to me that was forever.

Unfortunately, that early memory is as close as anyone will come to seeing inside the man that Brown was. His parents are gone.

When all this surfaced [the accident], my mother had a stroke and it affected her mentally and we were overwhelmed with the care she had to have.

Billy's father would never know his son was a hero. He died the same year that the crash documents were declassified, and he was never notified. Barbra is glad that at least she lived to get the call from the Silent Heroes of the Cold War.

"Oh yeah, I am glad that this has surfaced and they are being recognized and honored," she said. "I wasn't angry or bitter; it was just so overwhelming for me at the time because I had everything on the plate that I could handle at the time."

Every year she provides flowers for Billy's birthday at his grave and she thinks about how her life would have been different if Billy had survived.

Oh my goodness, I would have had a brother, a sister-in-law, nieces and nephews. I have been an only child. That bothers me from time to time.

Courtesy of Farris family

Clayton D. Farris

Occupation:	Sergeant Flight Mechanic
Employer:	United States Air Force
DOB:	June 7, 1929
Age:	26
Marital status:	Married

Clayton Farris loved everything a young man should: Speed and joking around.

Every time Johanna Katherine Dorman, Clayton Farris' niece, looks in the mirror, there's a reminder of her uncle.

I have a little piece of lead in my face. A pencil from Clayton's pocket stuck me in the face when he picked me up. I think I was three. A little tiny black mark where the lead went in left a little tiny black mark. It's on the cheek.

When she sees that little black mark, she thinks about the time Clayton handcuffed her to a coffee table, or how he asked her to whistle through her swollen tonsils. No one was safe from his jostling.

When he was a teenager, he was with his brother Charles out there sickling the yard and found a frog and brought it into the house. She [mother] saw the frog and went ape running out into the yard. He [Clayton] put it in her dishwater and got her to come back in the house. When she went back to washing dishes it jumped out and she fluttered all over the house when she saw it. Ha, ha, ha!

Clayton knew what he wanted to do when he grew up. He would look up at the planes in the sky and say "he was full of fly," meaning flying was his passion. But his joking nature took a grave toll on his dream.

When he joined the Air Force, they discovered that he had a disability.

He didn't get to be a pilot because when he was in Sunday school his teacher hit him in the ear with the Bible and busted his eardrum. That is the reason he couldn't fly the planes himself. But he could still fly. It kept him from being the pilot that he wanted to be. But I think that when he was up in the air the pilots would still let him fly.

As a training navigator, he would often have to drive from San Antonio to his home in Emerson. It was a drive that should have taken 12–14 hours back then, but Clayton drove like he was flying.

When he was on the ground he didn't think about going fast, but back then there wasn't any speed limits. He made it home from San Antonio to Emerson, Iowa in about 5 or 6 hours.

At home, he had a special message for Katherine.

He was a sweetheart. As a child he would always say, when I grow up, I will marry you. When he got married, it just about killed me.

Ten months after Clayton married Janet, Katherine was living with her mother in the little town of Wallet, Iowa, not far from Emerson.

We were baking pies to take to the locker. We didn't have home freezers. Everyone could go to the one building with the locker. We had just come back and the little TV was on and it said something about a plane crash there near Vegas somewhere. My mother said out of the blue: 'Clayton was on that plane,' but she didn't really know.

The tension and worry was very hard on her mother.

It was right after Sputnik went up and my mother had a nervous breakdown, and my grandmother called and told daddy to go home and tell my mother, be-

cause she didn't know what my mother would do. When he walked in, she immediately said, 'Clayton was on that plane, wasn't he?' The answer was terrifyingly simple and undeniable: 'Yes, he was.' It was the kind of answer that could make a mother collapse.

At the funeral, it was clear how much Clayton's life had impacted people around the world.

It was my heart and momma's heart. When we went to the church in Emerson, the church had flowers from all over the world.

But since it was a closed casket, all there was to look at was the American flag draped over it. It was a terrible image that burned into Katherine's mother's mind.

Till the day she died she hated the American flag, because it was over her son's body. It was over his casket.

The rest of her family tried to honor him. Another of Clayton's nieces, Caleela Danley, remembers her uncle's legendary story that was passed down through the generations.

All my life I have heard the stories about this plane crash, but never knew any of the details surrounding the crash. I contacted the newspaper; however I was only given the story that they printed.[12]

Most of his closest family members passed away without ever knowing the truth. Danley recalled: "My grandmother and her brother are both gone now and we are the only ones left behind." But Farris's vibrant personality lived on through his sister, Katherine Cotton.

Interestingly enough, Clayton's and my personality were very much the same. We both liked to kid around and laugh a lot and have fun.

Most memorable through the years was that Clayton's vibrancy was replaced with his mother's unimaginable suffering.

When Clayton was killed, his mother went through all

the stages of having lost a son. Most were normal, but her anger was totally multiplied. She blamed the Air Force, the government . . . anyone she could think to blame.

Danley continued:

When the first astronauts walked on the moon, instead of rejoicing like the world, she wondered why her son had received no accolades. 'After all', Ola Ferris, Clayton's mother, said 'He had given his life for his country.'

Margaret Farris wrote to the Silent Heroes of the Cold War:

Everything that I have been told, everything that I ever learned about the entire thing, my grandmother went to her grave never knowing the true story. Clayton was her baby. She was in a terrible car wreck several years later and until she died, she was bedridden with paralysis, caused by the auto accident. It was as if she had no will to live. She just simply never accepted that her son had been killed. I hope she knows now that we do care and that you wonderful people in Nevada, making sure more people know what they did. I thank you again.[13]

"Considering what I know about everything now," Farris wrote,

It's really hard to say, considering the number of people on the plane, but they should have got the families together and explained what the situation was and what they were doing. Did it really affect the country that much? I don't think so. My grandmother always made a comment that it was such secrecy, they just never knew. I don't think it was that big a secret. Hardly anybody knows about it unless you are a family member. My personal opinion, I think they should have told them.

*I can remember my grandmother; I remember her
talking about it. My grandfather, he was one of those
guys who just didn't talk very much. Both grandparents went to their grave not knowing. They did get to
bury his body and that was good.*

They weren't told very much.

"He was the navigator on the plane," Katherine recalled, now 66 years old.

*He was sitting between the pilots, the pilot and the co-
pilot. When they hit, something in the back of the plane
broke loose and he went right through the plane with
the box and that is about all they would tell us. When
it came out that it was top-secret and that they said
that there were scientists on it, it was stopped there.
Nothing else was said.*

Now that she knows the scope of what Clayton was
involved in, she is proud.

*We wondered if he knew the importance of the people
who he was flying and stuff like that. We wondered
what the scientists were doing.*

But what really mattered was that he was doing what
he loved. She doesn't harbor the same ill will that her
grandmother did. That's the difference a generation of
suffering can make.

*It really doesn't matter what they were doing, they
loved their country. They were doing what they loved
to do and if something like this should happen, they
died doing what they loved. I know Clayton loved the
Air Force. He loved to fly. He would see the planes and
said I am going to do that. I am going to fly.*

Now that she knows, she says, "It fills in a lot of
empty spaces."

She says that the same knowledge wouldn't have
made a difference for her grandmother, even if her son
were recognized as a hero.

I don't think it would have because that was her baby boy and I don't think even telling her that he was a hero would have mattered. They couldn't have said anything more that would have helped her any because she was in a state of depression from then on.

A generation later she is also under the impression that America isn't making these kinds of sacrifices anymore.

I think it is a sad situation. The person [pilot in covert operations] is out there; it is top-secret and it is a hard situation. But now days, it is all over the news. We don't have any top-secret things anymore.

Danley admires Clayton so much that she named her son after him, with the hope of keeping his memory close. But sadly, her son Clayton is nearly non-existent in her life, also. "I don't know what the deal is with him. I haven't seen him except when he passes by in the car." She can't wait until the day she can join her uncle.

It still kind of chokes me up, because one day I will see him because I know he is up there in heaven.

Courtesy of Fasolas family

Guy R. Fasolas

Occupation: 2nd class Flight Attendant
Employer: United States Air Force
DOB: July 7, 1934
Age: 21
Marital status: Single

In Guy's obituary, his brother recalled them passing pleasant country days as children, like floating in the irrigation canal near their grandparents' home in Nephi, Utah.

In Nephi, they helped their grandparents take care of the town park and cemetery. They would often play in the park with the sprinklers late at night. In the heat of the hot Utah nights, they would take turns, one standing at a sprinkler head in the desolate park and one standing at the sprinkler's controls. Guy would sometimes be the one who would crouch next to the sprinkler head. With the water turned off, he would reach down and turn the spout away from himself. At any moment his brother would turn on the spigot and it would start to spray, and Guy would run as fast as he could through the dark night before the sprinkler could make its rotation and spray him. It would inevitably get him, as he hoped.

There was also a deserted rail spur near their home and Guy figured out that he could let some of the air out of his car tires and drive along the rail spur that ran up the streets of the town. In their own minds, that was their way of rebelling against the law, because the law frowned on it.

Guy went to school in Nephi, too, and graduated from

Juab High School. Soon after graduation, he joined the United States Air Force. He was assigned to the Military Air Transport Service (MATS). Along his path to adulthood he also became a priest in the Aaronic Priesthood of the Nephi Third Ward. That's how he was identified in his obituary. He was buried in the Bluff Cemetery in Nephi, Utah.[14]

In a letter of condolence to Guy's mother on November 23, 1955, Major Ralph E. Bullock wrote that Guy lived up to the standards and traditions of the Air Force in all respects.

His likable personality was compounded with intelligence, common sense and a sincere interest in his fellow man. He always performed his duties as a Flight Traffic Specialist in an outstanding manner. The characteristics gained him the respect and admiration of his fellow man. His hobby of building model airplanes gained the interest of the airmen living with him in his barracks and they spent many idle hours together working on the airplanes.

Guy was flying with his regular crew on a scheduled transport mission from Burbank International Airport in California to Indian Springs. At 8:05 a.m. on November 17th, after flying in instrument weather conditions, his pilot reported to Nellis AFB, Nevada, by radio, advising that he had visual reference to the ground. They were not heard from again until the wreckage was sighted high on Mount Charleston.[15]

There is no such evidence in the crash documents. This false piece of information is likely the last the family heard of their son also.

Along with the letter came a certificate of Honorable Service stating that he died while in the service of our country as a member of the United States Air Force.

The rest of Guy Fasolas' short life seems to be long

lost. Silent Heroes of the Cold War researcher Miriam Kennedy followed up on the family name many years later to try to find his relatives. She sent a letter to librarian Bruce Lloyd asking for help.

Lloyd found a July 2003 newspaper article through the International Genealogy Index by searching for the last name only. At some point Fasolas' dad left Utah, but no one knew where he went. His mother died there in Nephi, where she once ran a dry-cleaning business. His mother's former business partner and the business partner's daughter are said to be somewhere in Arizona. The family has all but disappeared, most likely without ever knowing the truth.

John H. Gaines

Occupation: Lab Technician
Employer: United States Air Force
DOB: October 4, 1932
Age: 23
Marital status: Married

Courtesy of Gaines family

As short, obscure obituaries began to appear in newspapers across the nation for the accident victims of November 17, 1955, an obituary on December 2, in Ripley, Tennessee, appeared for John H. Gaines:

The Enterprise *reported that Air Force Sergeant John H. [Jack] Gaines of Woodville, 23, perished in the crash of an Air Force transport in the Charleston Mountain near Las Vegas. The plane was flying from Burbank, Calif., to the Atomic Energy Commission's Nevada Proving Ground.*

He graduated from Ripley High School and entered the Air Force in 1950. He re-enlisted February 1954 for another four years and planned on making the Air Force his career.[16]

That was it. Among the many interesting facts the paper could have included if the reporter were aware is that Gaines was originally discharged from the military exactly one year before his death, Nov. 17, 1954. He had re-enlisted, he told his family, because he couldn't find a job. Area 51, a top-secret project, was a strange place for a person who was hard-up for work to end up. Even today much of his life remains a mystery.

At the time of his death, Gaines had only been married a year-and-a-half to his wife, Wilma. They had a newborn daughter and he had just moved the new family to Burbank. The day of the accident he told her he didn't have to go back to work that day, but he decided to go anyway.

"You see these movies where they come and knock on your door [to tell you about someone's death]? Well, that is exactly what had happened. For a while I didn't have any information except for what they said on the TV," the 74-year-old Wilma recalled.

It was supposed to be the start of a new life for the newlyweds with a bright future ahead, but it ended as quickly as it had begun.

I came back home. I had this three-month-old baby. I started working at the old [USAF] personnel office, so I knew a lot of people there and that helped. But I hope you have never had to go through anything so bad that your heart hurts. My heart actually hurt. I was so young I didn't know how to cope with something like that.

She moved on, falling in love with, and marrying, her high school friend. But fifty years later, the questions were still burning deep inside, and not just for her, but for their daughter, too.

I don't think that's fair, I think I deserve an explanation and certainly Babs does. It was all very, very secretive. They interviewed people all over his home town about his character but they never actually told me anything.

Her daughter Barbara (Babs) Gaines Mikel, tried to piece together her mother's few memories to create a picture of her father.

I have had a stepfather all of these years and so I have been reluctant to ask a lot of questions. He was from Ripley, Tennessee, a rural farm area. He had a brother and two sisters. That's what Barbara remembers today.

Gaines' brother passed away and his sister has severe Alzheimer's, so Babs' mother, who knew Gaines for only a few years, is her only source of information about her father.

There is one important memory that she did share with her daughter: "I met Jack, June 24, 1953, in a small town near here, at the Masonic celebration," she recalled of the day she met her former husband. The night they met is still fresh in her mind. It was in a town on the Alabama-Florida border, aptly named Florala. Every year there is a celebration that hasn't changed much in 100 years. "They had square dancing in the streets and vendors."

That night she left the shirt factory where she worked with two girlfriends to go to the celebration.

This was in the evening. Those boys were walking behind us so we started talking and then we got some sandwiches and went down to the lake. And he got my address.

He was very tall, handsome, very nice, quiet, an extremely neat person. He had dark brown eyes and a crew cut. I was twenty years old. This was just two young kids. One thing that we did on Christmas, we were at a restaurant the day before Christmas Eve, and he wanted to know if I wanted to come with him to meet his parents.

She went with him even though she knew she would get in trouble for not going to work. She said that was probably not the best choice, but it paid off when they were married in May 1954.

She didn't mind being married to someone who did secret work.

It wasn't bad, because knowing the kind of person he was. He was very dedicated to his work and they had asked him to be secretive, but it was not a problem.

What she did know was that he was doing something different than the other men on that flight. He was a medic who worked in a laboratory, where they did blood work. But he was also outside a lot, she remembered, because he would get so dirty out there in the middle of nowhere, wherever it was.

He had the most underwear of anyone I ever saw because he said it was so dusty.

He liked to square dance, we did that a few dates. Back in those days you went to movies, we didn't have a TV. His sister had one in Texas, a little tiny thing. He was a little bit on the nervous side. Maybe that's not the right word. He wasn't boisterous.

I still get nervous when I get into this kind of stuff. He loved hamburgers and he loved strawberry preserves. He had both of these the day before he was killed. This was a very excruciatingly painful thing.

For his daughter Babs, it was also the kind of thing she could never forget, no matter how hard she tried. Every time she tried to think back, there was a big empty hole where this generous, loving father once was. "All I was ever told was that he was on a plane that hit the top of a mountain out in Nevada. That is all I ever knew and that is all mother really knew," Babs recalled.

Ya, I thought they should have told a lot more. But after forty or fifty years, I just never really thought about it. I thought he was flying to work and everything and I didn't realize, I thought it was just like a military base.

What's amazing is what the daughter didn't know.

Very surprised to find out he was part of a secret mission. I have always been very proud that he was in the military, but to be involved in that project, I was very proud of him that he was at that level, trusted that much to be included in that type of project.

This daughter's life took a 180-degree turn when her father died, a life that she longed to have despite how young she was.

The memory of John Gaines seemed destined to fade away. One of John's sisters had a picture of him on the wall, his mother recalled. But one day she realized her children didn't know who he was, and since she didn't have much to say about him either, she took it down and put it away in a chest. That's the last she remembers of the picture, locked away like the facts of the crash, put away like the memory of what Bab's life could have been.

"I realized that (if he hadn't died) I would not have lived in Andalusia most of my life. There is a lot of difference between Alabama and California," Babs recalled in her southern drawl when she thinks about how she would have led a California-dreaming kind of life if her father had not died.

Though the facts of the accident were finally revealed, the damage had already been done. Bab's life would remain changed forever. And the heroism of her father was only barely salvaged.

Courtesy of Hanks family

Fred Farrar Hanks

Occupation: Camera technician
Employer: Hycon Manufacturing Company
DOB: August 26, 1920
Age: 35
Marital status: Married

Fred F. Hanks had a huge family, the kind of family with so many relatives you know at least one of them is destined for greatness. Fred was the third oldest in a line of ten children: Earl, Laverne, Helen, Grace, Glena, Glen, Paul, Betty, and Billy.

Back home near Amarillo, Texas, Betty Jean Hanks remembers the little things that made this brother an even bigger hero for any little sister. One time he had to drive the truck with a broken steering wheel, another time, how brave he was when he had to put their dog Peewee to sleep. There was the day when he was ready to start a family, going to the hitching post dressed in a smart white jacket. He was the only one of the ten siblings to graduate high school, and that wasn't all that made Fred different from the rest.

Fred loved music. He had music for everything, to shave by, to take a bath with music.

It wasn't just any kind of music, though, his brother Billy Hanks recalled.

Fred was a funny guy. He liked classical music and the rest of my family liked country music. He wasn't out of the same bunch that we were. But it seemed like he was always there when something happened. He showed up at the darndest times.

One of those 'darndest' times was during a play his

brother Billy was in. His parents couldn't show up, but out of nowhere Fred suddenly appeared in the audience.

Like the other victims of the accident, he was pretty good at keeping his family insulated from his work.

We just figured he was doing something with cameras. He was an aerial photographer in the Air Force. Everywhere he went he always had a camera with him, always taking pictures.

At home, his sister Betty Jean Hanks remembers the strong instinct he had to capture hidden things on film.

He came home on leave one time and I had a little old cat and my Grandpa Hanks come from Texas and he brought us tamales from a thermos, and the cat wanted to play in the thermos and Fred tried to catch a picture of that cat all day long trying to play in that thermos so he could take a picture.

This desire to document secretive things through images shows how well he was adapted to the overall mission of his job and the U-2. But while his job was to work on capturing hidden secrets in the Cold War, little did he know he would become one of those secrets himself.

He was a liaison pilot, Billy remembered. *He flew gliders over Europe and Korea, taking pictures. He was shot down twice. The wings on his uniform show it. The last time I saw him was in 1945.*

In 1945, Fred once again showed up out of nowhere. He somehow got word that Billy was about to make what Fred considered a mistake. Out of high school, Billy was scheduled to enter the Marine Corps. It was important enough for Fred to make his way to the recruiting office when Billy was signing up.

My brother showed up and said you are not going in the Marine Corps; you are going in the Air Force.

That was the last time Billy saw his brother. The next

time he heard his brother's name, Billy was 18, stationed at a base east of San Diego, California.

I had just pulled a 14-day tour of KP duty and we lived in Alpine. We were listening to 'Gunsmoke' on the radio and it came over the radio that there had been a plane crash. They gave out all the victims' names and I thought I heard my brother's name.

But Billy wasn't sure and just continued to go about his business. Then his first sergeant came by and told him to report to the commanding officer.

He told me to get a hold of Hycon Manufacturing Company. He told me Fred had been in a plane crash and that there were no survivors. The company Fred worked for sent me $500 to go home for the funeral.

On the other hand, his brother-in-law, who lived in Nevada, actually tried to get to the actual crash site.

What do you do when the government tells you 'no'? My brother-in-law was at the site and he and my sister told me that the [military police] said that if they crossed the line, they would shoot 'em; that is what my sister told me.

Fred was part of the glue that had held this large family together; the loss and mystery surrounding Fred's death seemed to dissolve that glue.

I never questioned it, I don't know why but I didn't. My mother passed away three years before, December 1953 and when Fred passed away our family went in all different directions.

Indeed, the government and its contractors knew much more about Fred Hanks. It was as if his work became his family. Denny Thatcher, also a Hycon employee, felt compelled to tell the story that Fred's family had never heard for the sake of all Americans and the victims of the Silent Heroes of the Cold War:

Fred was deployed as a night photographer during the

Korean War in 1951 as part of the US Air Force 162nd Tactical Reconnaissance Squadron. His unit used equipment manufactured by Hycon Manufacturing Company of Pasadena, California.

As a technical Representative of Hycon, I was sent to Japan and Korea for support, training, and maintenance of the A-14 Aerial Film Magazine. The USAF camera repair personnel were not trained in electronics so I established a special school at the Far East Air Material Command [FEAMCOM] at Tachikawa, Japan, not far from Tokyo.

We also set up a maintenance depot and overhaul facility to service equipment being shipped in from Korea. Me and Fred did it all ourselves so we became pretty close as friends and co-workers.

When his squadron was transferred from Japan to Tague Air Base in Korea, Fred and I really had our hands full. We repaired cameras in a Quonset hut along side the dusty runway. The dirt would pour into the primitive tent. That meant we were always inspecting, maintaining, and overhauling the critical camera systems.

Fred was a real breath of fresh air being such a dedicated and experienced person. I knew I could persuade him to knock on Hycon's door when he left the Air Force. He did just that and my recommendation for Fred to our company management led him to be hired immediately.

He got married in Ohio to Betty and moved right out to California. They enjoyed their rustic little home up in a tree-covered canyon near Sierra Madre, California.

But their happiness was not for long. The call had come into the company that the aircraft Fred Hanks and Hycon's consultant Harold C. Silent were on had crashed on Mount Charleston in Nevada.

Because of my being such a close friend and co-work-er of Fred's, I was asked if I would go up to their home in the foothills and tell Betty. That was the most difficult task I had ever been called upon to do. Betty had become such a good and close friend. I knew I had to gain my composure and pass along what little information I had. What a brave and wonderful woman she was and she made it through the ordeal just fine.

Betty has since remarried a wonderful man whom she had known back in Ohio and who also had come to California to work for Hycon. Bob Matchett is the gentleman's name.

Fred had only been married seven months when he died. His family didn't meet Betty until his funeral. Thatcher recalled the meeting.

She was telling me that they took their honeymoon in the Grand Canyon and went on a mule train ride and enjoyed a lot when they were down there.

Fred's sister, Betty Jean Hanks, was relieved when they heard the story.

I was delighted that we finally got to know what he was doing. We had no idea that that was what he was working on.

Billy also had no idea what his brother was doing until volunteers of the Silent Heroes of the Cold War contacted him. The words over the phone hit hard.

I was kind of proud and it made me feel kind of proud because many people have said the U-2 stopped World War III. In a way it surprised me and in a way it didn't, because he was quite a guy.

Now Billy is part of another family, one of long-lost and forgotten heroes.

Yeah, it kind of makes me mad. Who I really felt for were the kids of those people that died. When it hap-

pened, I talked to three of them and they were six or seven years old and it upset them real bad. It's just something like the government does these things and don't want you to know about them.

Billy used to haul goods from the "secret" Area 51 to Los Alamos, so the whole idea that this accident needed to be a secret was a total farce to him. They were Americans and just like Fred, Billy says his family would have protected the project, too. The government could have trusted them he says.

I think they could have explained a little bit and not just shut everybody off. The rescuers that went up there, they are heroes, too. But one of the rescuers said that after they got everyone down the military had a chow set up and fed them steaks, but charged them $3.75. Why would the government do that? They risked their lives going after those people and then to be treated like they were. That is being a hero; they risked their lives going after them in that kind of weather and situations.

What could have been a story of heroes and a source of pride was hidden for too many years and left a bad taste in Billy's mouth.

I think they should have at least let us know something was going on. After they declassified everything, why didn't they tell us then? Why didn't the government try to contact us? Right now I have a pretty low opinion of our government. I am 70 years old. I have COPD now and I had to quit work and I have a house to pay for and I am drawing social security but I don't have enough money to pay all of my payments. But the government doesn't help me because they say I made too much money. Our government thinks that everyone in the world ought to have a government like we got, but I don't think so.

Courtesy of Hruda family

Richard J. Hruda

Occupation: Engineer
Employer: Lockheed
DOB: September 30, 1918
Age: 37
Marital status: Married

One of the first words Richard Hruda taught his son was "Torque converter."

"Here was this little kid, barely able to walk, and going around the house saying "Torque converter, torque converter," Kenneth Hruda says. He was the son who spoke those words at the urging of his father. Eventually there were also words Richard didn't want his children to know.

When we did hear what he said, we got in trouble. Code words. One of the projects he was working on was called project 'Flying Submarine' and I told one of my dad's friends once in front of my dad, 'There is no way you can make a submarine fly. It's too heavy.' He looked terrified; he turned around and walked off.

Life was a balancing act for Richard Hruda, testing the bounds of engineering principles and struggling to keep work and family separated as required for national security. Though he was a primary engineer for the U-2, his children believed he never witnessed the flight of the actual masterpiece he worked on. The doomed flight of November 17, 1955, would have been the day he would see his life's legacy. Kenneth believes it was a mission to see the second test flight of the U-2, though others say the U-2 had been flying for some time by that point.

Richard's legacy now lives through his children's

memory. The stories of Richard as a young man are gone forever, because his parents have passed away. But his children hold tight to the memories of the time he spent with them, the few moments when their father was not consumed by work.

Richard's humble beginnings were at Chicago Trade Tech. He and his dad worked at a local screw company. One day Lockheed had some recruiters at the school. When Richard told them he was working for the screw company, the Lockheed recruiters knew immediately that they had their man. They told him they would pay for the rest of his schooling and then he would be expected to show up in California to work for Lockheed when he graduated. Richard's son, Kenneth, remembered:

During WWII, working for Lockheed in Burbank, he was working for 50 cents an hour and they made him do all the drilling holes, riveting. They wanted these engineers to have hands-on experience. My mother got a job in the tool crib earning 75 cents an hour. And so here is a guy with four years of college and he got 50 cents an hour and his wife was earning more. They couldn't afford a car, so they rode around on a scooter and lived in a studio apartment.

Once they had children, their combined $1.25 hourly wage wasn't enough to support their family, Kenneth said.

When I was young I thought we were poor. We couldn't even afford to live in the house in the summer. We had to pack up and live in the woods for three months. My dad was extremely conservative and I thought we were poor.

His dad's frugality became his son's frugality. "My job was to sweep the sidewalk and the driveway. I could never figure out how anyone drove up their driveway without sweeping it. But that is how I got a nickel a week. My kids suffered just about as much when they were growing up."

One of my dad's hobbies was investing in the stock market. He would come home from work and tear out the stock listings from the Los Angeles Times *and he maintained hand-drawn graphs on the ones he had bought. Being just a kid, I wanted a reason to talk to my dad and so I decided that I needed to talk to him about what he was interested in. I grabbed the* Los Angeles Times *and tried to learn what I was looking at. Being that my allowance was rather low, I found a stock called Bizreal Oil that was selling for a quarter of a dollar and when he came home from work, I had my page opened up to it ready to show him. He said 'that's a penny stock; you don't want to have anything to do with that.'*

But Kenneth kept bothering his dad about it until he said,

We will buy $10 worth and that seemed like 'wow!' I ran in the bedroom and got my piggy bank. I had $3.20 and he said 'no, we will do this on paper'. So we put down $10 worth.

Eventually Kenneth's investment was worth a whopping $75.00 on paper. One day his father's friends came over to play cards. "They would talk about how much money they lost in the stock market, and my dad said, 'you want some hot stock tips, you gotta talk to my son over there.'" Kenneth sits in silence after telling that story. It's a silence like only a son can appreciate reliving the memories with a father.

Another way Kenneth pried his way into his father's secretive and busy life was by interrupting him when he was looking at aircraft blueprints.

My dad hauled blueprints home all the time. I am pretty sure none of them were critical. One of the things I

*was told is that my dad redesigned the landing gear
on the U-2. Only one wheel in the middle.*

The old U-2 nose wheel was adapted from other aircraft and Kenneth says his father was the one who decided it was just too heavy the way that it was.

Kenneth was used to talking to his dad about these blueprints. Long before ever working on the U-2 design, Richard had some blueprints scattered on his bed one night and was looking at them when his son came in to talk to him. Kenneth remembers that he was only in first grade.

*You know how you want to talk to your dad. One day,
he [dad] had a gangplank [stairway] for an airplane
that they had mounted on a jeep chassis so they could
move it up to the aircraft without pushing it by hand.
My dad was trying to figure out how to lighten the
gangplank so that it wouldn't overload the jeep chassis
and flip over.*

"I was real proficient with Tinker Toys," Kenneth says. "And I went back to my bedroom and built a gangplank structure and showed him what was wrong."

Kenneth says his father went to school for civil engineering, originally hoping to design and build bridges for the railroad. His love of engineering, however, allowed him to work on the cutting edge of flight engineering related to national security.

*Way back then, these guys were just civil engineers
building aircraft. One of the important things was
stress testing. He taught two or three classes a week,
one was stress analysis.*

This field elevated Richard from a poor engineer who lived in the woods to a top-earning position.

*One time we were watching a thing on TV about
Chuck Yeager breaking the sound barrier and I wasn't
too impressed at the time. The report said that Yeager*

was paid the 'fabulous' sum of $15,000 a year and I remember my dad saying 'Humph! I make more than he does.' By the amount of money he was making back then I realized he was a valued engineer.

Despite the earnings, Richard never lost his frugal nature.

Joy Cunniff, Richard's daughter, remembered that he rarely went on business trips or family vacations and he rode his bike to work because the family only had one car.

In some ways, his father's business connections offered experiences that his children otherwise might not have had. There was a private ski lodge in the Los Angeles Mountains where the engineers would all meet and talk about projects and ski. One day while skiing, Kenneth hit a 4-foot wide tree and broke a ski.

My dad, being really cheap, had bought Army surplus skis. I saw a receipt for $2.50 a pair. He pulled out a pair of these and got the bindings; here was a 4 foot 11 inch kid with 7 foot skis. I couldn't even do a kick turn, but after I grew into them, I was good.

He says he also gained something very important from his father, a work ethic, which often kept his father away from the family. Kenneth didn't understand it growing up, but later his mother explained how much even the little bit of time they spent together meant to his father.

At the time I was ignored a lot; but after he died, my mom told me he said, 'You know what; it is fun to go skiing with Ken.

Kenneth remembers a certain day at school when he was eight or nine years old. "I got called into the office and told my dad was missing. I got sent home and the house was full of people. And that is pretty much what I remember. The other thing I remember is that people were hoping he would be okay for four days."

Joy Cunniff, remembers that their mother had a bad feeling the night before.

I do remember one thing that she did say. She knew that there was something wrong before the people came to the house. She had had a dream where she was at a gathering and had a glove on her left hand and someone asked why, and she said it was because her wedding ring was gone.

I remember taking a rabbit's foot and talking to my girlfriend down the street and wishing on the rabbit's foot that he was going to be all right and at the time they were hoping for survivors. At the first they thought there were survivors but after that they thought it was the metal flashing.

That light was not made by survivors flashing signal mirrors, as they had hoped.

After that everything was pretty much unsettled. I re-member, we must have had a funeral, and I remember my paternal grandmother was pretty upset because we didn't have an open coffin and that was because of the accident. I know that grandmother didn't talk to my mother from that point on, which kind of put that division between the family and that is one reason why I didn't know that much either.

Because the bodies were so mangled and I know my father requested that he be cremated. He was not a strong religious person. He was a Baptist and he never went back to church after he was 18. I know that. And my mom took us to church but he never went.

Unlike the other families, the Hrudas weren't about to bury the truth without a fight.

Our family sued the government. The plane shouldn't have been flying in those mountains because it wasn't on the way to White Sands, New Mexico. Being from an aviation community, we had friends of the inven-

*tor of the automatic pilot. The flight was way, way off
course. Kenneth actually believed.*

*He told us he was going to White Sands, so he kind
of told us a lie, too.*

The lawsuit didn't provide the answers they were
looking for, but Kenneth doesn't resent the lawsuit or
the lack of information.

*They couldn't tell us the real story. We were told that
the plane was going to White Sands. In 1955 Groom
Lake did not exist. You gotta feel sorry for the government. They are just trying to keep something under
wraps there.*

*I think it is necessary that we keep these secrets when
they are relevant like that. Knowing what I know now,
they had loyal employees because they were way off
course and they couldn't admit that they lied, so they
paid.*

The family was awarded around $100,000 and Ken-
neth doesn't feel bad about it. "Not really, it made it
so that our family actually made it. We lost a huge in-
come."

And the questions remained until one day an engineer
with loose lips stopped by.

*One of the engineers happened to be over at the house
a year-and-a-half later. We saw a U-2 fly over and he
told me to be proud when I saw that plane fly.*

Once another engineer even showed Kenneth a video
of the U-2 taking off. That raises the question: If there
were videos circulating, why did they have to keep the
death of a family member secret?

Over the years, Kenneth has been able to piece together bits of his father's role in the U-2 development.

He was the lead engineer for what is known as the
center section of the U-2, nose cone, and tail cone, and
the wings on it, and you get an airplane. He was in-

volved in the center section where the pilot sat, where the surveillance system sat.

This knowledge has given him a connection to his father that he's been able to carry proudly with him. Piecing together his dad's work started very young. Kenneth remembers that when he was a Boy Scout, he went on a trip to Edwards Air Force Base. He asked a man there if they had any U-2s and the man asked why he wanted to know. Kenneth said his father who was killed had worked on them.

One of the officers standing out on the ramp heard the conversation. "So he took me over to a hangar." The little 8-year-old-boy stood in the giant doorway and there before him were "at least a half dozen U-2s stacked in that hangar, the wings overlapping each other." Even now as an adult he says it with a sense of awe.

Today, each of Richard's children cope with the reality of their father's mysterious death a little differently. The scars run deep for Larry Hruda.

I wanted so badly to have a dad to do things with. To this day, I have no interest in sports and have never been any good at anything but snow skiing. I guess it's due to the lack of a male role model in my life.[17]

Larry would ask his mother all the time about his father. Finally he wrote to the Silent Heroes of the Cold War:

All of my life, I have been told a specific story about my father and what he did. It was always the exact same story and nobody ever deviated from it. Sure I would ask questions, but Mom never really answered them. Now I see that it was a nice, neat prefabricated story that I was fed to keep me from prying into his life.

For his daughter, Joy, the news of her father's role in the U-2 reopened old internal wounds.

I went to the Silent Heroes of the Cold War website

and started reading things and found that I couldn't read all the pages all at once. I found that I would read them and be so upset I would be in tears because it brought back a lot that I didn't know. But I didn't know the specifics and the specifics kind of brought it out. And what was difficult was I had no one to share it with.

My main hurt right now is seeing my husband and my daughter's relationship and knowing that I missed all that. My mother must have done a pretty good job of raising us so that it wasn't an all encompassing thing.

She says her mother felt alone and the grieving process will never fully be completed. Not knowing what happened pushed her mother away from the family, Joy said.

She went immediately into college and into a career because she always had that fear in the back of her mind that she needed something to fall back on in case something ever happened. In case something 'like what happened to my father ever happened again, like a sudden and unexpected disappearance.'

Their mother had heard of the place where Richard had died, but no one had actually ever pointed it out to her. She had even driven by the area once, not even realizing how that mountain would affect her life. According to Joy, only a few days after her mother had driven past that mountain, she found out it was the site of her son's death.

Rodney H. Kreimendahl

Occupation: Engineer
Employer: Lockheed
DOB: August 3, 1917
Age: 38
Marital status: Married

Courtesy of Kreimendahl family

There are two ways to remember Rodney Kreimendahl:

According to his son Stephen, "He had a real lust for life, very brilliant, talented at building things."

Bryan Kreimendahl, another son, also remembers that side of his father, as well as a softer, second side. "I remember my father as a loving man even though he took the strap to me more than once."

In a letter to the Silent Heroes of the Cold War, Bryan Kreimendahl wrote:

I can remember one specific incident that spoke to his nature. I was sick with the flu and I ended up throwing up right on top of the floor furnace. Can you imagine cleaning that up? My father asked me angrily why I had not picked a better spot. A few moments later he came and hugged me and apologized for his outburst and told me he loved me.

His children remember that Rodney Kreimendahl came from a broken home in Westfield, Massachusetts and his love for airplanes grew from his admiration of Charles Lindberg. He spent much of his time building model airplanes as a young man and won several awards. He was also an Eagle Scout.

Rodney's family couldn't afford to send him to college, so he became a draftsman for Chance-Vought. Eventually he won a scholarship to Northeastern University. When

Lockheed went headhunting prior to World War II, Rodney was recruited as a structural designer and sent to Burbank. That's where his wife-to-be was secretary for the lead stress man on the project.

After World War II, Rodney wanted to be a part of a new class of flight racing called the Goodyear racers, or "midgets" as his kids called them, because they were so small. Lockheed already had started to design a plane to race in the class, which was named the Cosmic Winds. Rodney couldn't get on board that development team because the group already had enough members, "so my dad started up a new group, which put in $1 per week," Bryan recalled.

"My dad did the configuration and all the design work on the midget racer which, when my mother was asked, 'what should we name it?' she came up with the name 'Shoestring,' because it was built on a shoestring." Rodney and his team did everything they could to complete the plane, but it was missing one important part—the engine. In 1949, they got it off the ground when Bob Downey, the first race pilot, loaned them an engine.

My father would take my brother and me to the airport on weekends to watch it fly. That was the beginning of a long racing career that still carries his spirit today.

In his spare time in 1954, Rodney started building a new home in Northridge for his growing family.

He bought an old woody, a 1941 Woody. They used to haul building materials and things back and forth to the house and I remember the Woody was painted pink and purple, a garish, outlandish looking thing.

Another thing they did together was join the YMCA's Indian Guides.

We won the 'highest flying' and the 'biggest kite' trophy one year. I was 'Little Red Fox' and he was 'Big Moose'. I think for any young boy a father is a hero.

That's without knowing what he did for a living. All they knew is that he worked for Lockheed. All this time, the children didn't even know what he was working on, let alone that it was top-secret.

"Nothing was ever talked about at home as far as work," Stephen recalled. Bryan remembers the closest they ever got to discussing dad's work was as he went out the door each day.

My father usually left for work before we were up in the morning. In those days people carpooled a lot and I can remember my mother had a little ditty she would sing as he walked out the door: Badge, bag [lunch], zipper [pants] . . .

But one day after singing the song, he didn't come back.

"As far as the day of the accident goes, I came home at five o'clock, approximately, which would be supper-time," remembered Stephen Kriemendahl, who was only twelve years old at the time.

And there were two people from, I want to say Red Cross, or Lockheed, sitting with my mom on the couch and she was crying. And I was shooed into the back bedroom and it was explained to me that there had been an accident; that an airplane was missing and they were searching for it and trying to find it. It took a while for them to find it, a week or so because there was a snowstorm.

It was quite a different experience for Bryan, who was younger.

On the day of the airplane crash all I can remember is that someone came and fetched me out of school and when I got home there were a lot of people in the house, mostly relatives, I imagine. I was told to go outside and play. It did not take long before I began to feel as if we, my mother, brother, and sisters were all different now.

Not a bad different, just different.

The young Bryan was thrust into a new world, one where he always seemed to be standing at the edge of a gaping hole in his life left by a missing father. He just kept waiting for his father to come back so he could fall into his arms.

Eventually, I became used to the idea that a life without father was the way it was going to be. My grandfather or uncle would take my brother and me to Father-Son banquets and such. A nice fellow from church, Dewit Casson, would take my brother and me to high school football games.

Bryan's admiration for his father was ingrained as a child, and he decided that one way to fill the emptiness in his life was to become like his father. That way he would always be with him.

Shortly after my father's death, I was on an outing with other young boys. One boy told me that if you saw a hay truck pass, made a wish, and did not look back to see the same hay truck again, the wish would come true. Shortly, a hay truck passed and I wished I could be just like my dad. I refused to look back and to this day I don't know if the wish came true or not. In some regards I hope it did not. During periods of uncertainty in my life where I have felt I needed a little help, I have repeated this "wish" technique.

Despite the fact that he never knew what his dad did, he did turn out a little like his father, working on Lockheed projects as well.

The emotions and pain that were so hard to express as a child are easier for Bryan now. He recalls that his mother found someone to finish the house in Northridge and they sold it, having never lived in it. That was just part of the unfinished business his father left behind: four children, a wife, house, and an airplane. Bryan reflected:

The whole experience was very hard on my mother and I am sure us kids did not make the situation better. She has told me how grateful she is for the help and guidance that was provided her from people within our church and relatives, primarily my grandfather. At the time of the crash my older brother was eleven, just coming of age, and the loss of my father perhaps had a more profound effect on him than me. My younger sister was seven. The youngest sister was only three and she never got to know anything of my father first hand. I think she is the one that has been the most affected. In the '50s, single parent households were not common. In today's world there are many young children that grow up knowing only one parent. We were never told what my father was working on but it was known that it was a top-secret project.

They got information through a slow trickle.

Anyway, in 1955, you didn't have the communication that you have today, you didn't have the mass media and the news where news just spreads like wildfire after the occurrence, Stephen pointed out.

Five years later, they got a big clue as to what he was working on.

When Gary Power's U-2 was shot down in 1960, my uncle told me that was the airplane my father was working on when he was killed. Today, I think that was just conjecture on my uncle's part, but he was correct. My mother told me recently that Kelly Johnson, also known as the father of Area 51, did come to our house a couple of times to talk with her but never mentioned what dad was working on.

The loss of his father continues to impact Stephen even decades later.

I didn't have the opportunity to get to know him in a

*more mature way; I would have loved to have had
that opportunity. I considered him a great guy and I
missed him a lot.*

By doing some similar work himself, Bryan learned
about his father. Stephen hasn't had that same luxury,
but he doesn't resent that the work was a secret.

*Yeah, that is just part of working in that part of the
game when you are working on a top-secret project
like that. You don't want the general public or your
enemies to know about it. You can't say anything. You
can't let your family know. That is just the nature of
the beast of that type of work. If he was a plumber
or carpenter or electrician, or something like that, of
course he could talk about his work all that he wanted
to. But in the context of his work, he could not. He
couldn't mention anything.*

Today Stephen knows.

*Hindquarters. That was my dad's expertise. You know
from the U-2, the design of the hindquarters of the U-2.*

There's no doubt life would have been different for
all the Kreimendahls if their father hadn't died. "Quite
a bit actually," Stephen remembers a very serious talk
with his mother about their life.

*My mom asked me several years ago, is there something
in your life that you wish had changed in regard to our
family? And I said the one thing I regretted is that you
never remarried, that there was never another man in
the house. I needed male guidance in the house. I had
nowhere to go to have male-type questions answered;
no one to be a confidant with. I missed that a lot, not
having that.*

While Bryan has come to terms with what his father
was doing on that flight, there was clearly something
even bigger missing, a sense of peace.

It has been so long now since my father's death that it

almost seems that it should have been no other way. As a matter-of-fact, November 17th would have come this year without much thought of the incident. You know, sometimes I have sat on top of a mountain and have thought how I could take a rock and throw it to the bottom. I could smash it into little bits if I wanted. But you know, in the end it will still be here and I will not.

Interestingly, what Rodney Kreimendahl may be best known for is the sum of the parts of a much more obscure, unique aircraft, than the U-2: "Shoestring," which carried its own secrets.

My father told me once that as a child making models that they would have to cut their own propellers. Dad understood prop design. We kept the racing prop in our hall closet and we were told never show it to anyone, Bryan said. He still has his father's original papers with the curve design that detailed the twist distribution for that propeller.

Though a fragile aircraft, Shoestring continues to carry the family's name across generations. In 1952, before he died, Rodney put Shoestring up for sale to build that bigger house in Northridge. The midget has been sold various times over the years, shipped back and forth across the country, but racing all the time.

Bryan proudly notes:

Shoestring's design is considered a classic of the era for this type of aircraft. The last owner of the Shoestring gave me a list of all the airplane's wins and claimed it to be: 'The aircraft with the most wins in aviation history.'

If only the developer were here to see it.

Courtesy of Marr family

William G. Marr Jr.

Occupation: Security
Employer: CIA
DOB: August 27, 1918
Age: 37
Marital status: Married

It's remarkable how ordinary William Marr's life appeared on the surface, despite the extraordinary work he was doing.

We loved to play bridge, we loved California and driving around and seeing the woods. The Muir woods, his widow, Sidney, *re-called. We traveled every other year. Every other year we would drive out to the coast and back.*

One of the things William looked forward to each fall was the opening of hunting season. He would go back to where he was raised on a Maryland tobacco farm and hunt with the tenant farmers. Their nickname for him was "Uncle Sam."

But returning to the farm once a year wasn't enough. There was something about William that needed satisfying. He gained a lot of pleasure working with something he could nurture, something beautiful for others to see, something that also helped him return to his roots and home as a farmer.

"He loved gardening," and not just gardening during the day," Sidney remembered. "He would garden late into the night." He would garden so late that "I would have to string a light out so he could see." She never questioned him even when it bordered on obsession.

We had a very small lot in Maryland. It was a new house and he was working on the yard and he decided that we would have dwarf fruit trees. He ordered them through catalogs and they kept coming and the mailman one day asked what are you doing with all these trees? He just didn't want to stop. That was his outlet. Because of the pressures of work, he loved to come home and garden. He put in a garden for his parents also. He was a very serious man, but he was fun, too.

Sidney understood his mindset better than others, possibly because she had worked for the FBI herself. "Every time you left the house, you had to call in," she said, presumably to let "them" know where you were going. Sidney and William met during his 16-year career with the FBI and were married in Salt Lake City, Utah, April 10, 1945.

Like most of the men in these pages, William had a rural upbringing. His elementary school education was in Brown, Maryland (Now upper Marlboro, Maryland) in a one-room school, which was unusual even at that time. People used a simple name for him "Bill"; a simple name for a man who was to have very complicated tasks. While in college at George Washington University, he worked in the office of J. Edgar Hoover, Director of the FBI, and attended school at night. He received his Bachelor's Degree in History and Political Science.

After sixteen years with the FBI, he started working for the CIA. "I would tell people he worked for the National Security Administration," Sidney recalled.

He was a great reader and he loved to write. Oh, personal things, he kept a diary. We didn't have e-mail and we didn't use the phone as freely as you do today. So he wrote letters.

But he didn't write about work; and if he did, all he said was that he "had a busy day at work," Sidney said.

The best, you couldn't find a better more principled, finer man than he was. He was a patriot and honest and just all the good qualities you would find in William Marr.

All she knew is that; then one day he flew out to California.

"It was so long ago. You are in such shock. The plane went down on a Thursday morning." At 11:00 at night her doorbell rang. When she opened the door, two agents were standing there.

One of whom I knew rather well came in and said they wanted to talk to me. They told me that they had not been able to reach the crash site and they would keep me advised. The next day was payday, they said we don't know how you are financially but we will come out first thing with a check and get it in the bank in case you need it. One of them stayed with me for two nights.

The CIA did something they didn't do for any of the other families. The CIA director made a personal visit to her in a private room.

Interesting, looking back, when they gave me the posthumous medal within the year of his death, no one was invited but me. They didn't include my family or anyone. I don't recall if there was anyone there. Maybe one or two people, but they were CIA people and then it was just the director and I and it was very quiet.

Sidney didn't know what her husband did that was so deserving of this visit, but the director placed the CIA's Intelligence Medal of Merit in her hand.

Financially, she was better off than some of the other families. William Marr was a forward-looking man and like the other men, very fiscally frugal. At one point, he told his wife that he considered stopping regular payments to his life insurance policy, since after all, he was still alive.

He had talked to me a couple of months before he died

*and said should we quit it [life insurance], but I said
'no,'* Sidney recalled. *And it was very helpful.*

It was not a lot, but my husband, he was very thought-ful; he took out mortgage insurance so that if he was killed, our mortgage was paid for. Right away (the insurance paid) $100 a month and then (somehow the payment dropped and it) was $60 a month.

What was an even bigger help was his work.

*He had worked for the government at that time for
over 20 years and that makes a difference if you are
younger and working for a company. I was in a better
position [than the other families] in that way.*

With their finances fairly stable, the challenge was keeping a strong sense of family. Sidney had two young boys at the time and it was hard to tell how they took it after explaining to them that their father wouldn't be back.

*It is hard to judge; looking back I expected too much
of them. I didn't wake them up until the next morning
and I was going to tell my husband's parents before it
came out in the newspapers. So I just told them that
their father's plane was down and we didn't know
what the outcome was going to be. I left someone with
them and told them that I needed to see grandmother
and grandfather.*

She remembers that, "The nine-year-old was almost stoic about it, but it impacted him more than the five-year-old because he was older." It took a while to sink in. "They cried, of course, but not that moment. They didn't really understand; it settled in later in the months following."

She tried to keep a sense of family about the house for the young boys.

*From that time on, I would invite families to the house.
That way they could interact with the fathers and
made it a more normal kind of thing.*

Sidney didn't ask any questions about what William was doing when he died. Her main goal was trying to keep the lines of communication open with her children, letting them know that talking about William Marr was not taboo.

We talked about their father from the very first day, and some people were very uncomfortable with that, but we discussed it, almost as if he were still living at some times.

She had a picture of him blown up that was taken a year before he died and hung it on the wall.

Well, you know the first time I really knew what he was working on was when Gary Powers' plane was shot down and one of the men said to me, 'I am not supposed to tell you this but that was Bill's baby.'

This wife of a CIA agent took her responsibility of national security and secrecy very seriously. "I didn't share that, no, no. I kept that to myself." Even though her children would have liked to have known, she kept it a secret until 1998. But why? "Little boys, they would be so pleased they would go out and tell everyone and since he (one of the men) said: 'I am not supposed to tell you this.' I didn't tell anyone."

Sidney thinks more people should respect the government's right to secrecy.

I don't think people appreciate the role that covert operations should play in our country. I think we talk too much in our country. I respect their right to keep it quiet. I had the choice of suing the government or accepting a certain amount [of money] each month.

She seemed mostly at peace with the government methods until they held the declassification ceremony in 1998. She was both elated by a recognition ceremony and confused by its seeming openness to an old project.

Several of the victims' families from the crash at Mount Charleston unknowingly crossed paths on that day in September 1998 during the declassification ceremony for the U-2. Little did they know there were documents that were declassified too. At the ceremony, panels of pilots, engineers, historians, policy-makers, and authors discussed the U-2's development, operations, and policy impact. At noon, the U-2 performed a commemorative flyover.

It was overwhelming; it was really beautifully done and inspiring and my son from New York said 'if I had any idea how wonderful this would be, I would have taken my children out of school and brought them,' Sidney recalled.

At Fort McNair, which is on the outskirts of Washington, DC, the army had a program and told us all about the U-2. After lunchtime they set up chairs outside facing one of the buildings, and they had all of the family members there on the front row and they did a memorial service, planes flew over and we were all given a posthumous medal.

The night before, Sidney was also invited to a reception at the aerospace museum with dignitaries and watched a movie about the U-2.

"It was a reception and we were allowed to walk around but it wasn't very personal," she remembered. She wandered through the crowds and even if anyone had read the newly declassified documents, few would probably know who her husband was or the role he played. Later, Sidney found that personal satisfaction, but not through a big government ceremony; instead, it was through that stranger Steve Ririe, who had sent her a copy of the crash documents. She read them closely.

I thought it was strange that they blocked out the names even when it was declassified. It didn't matter to me but I thought it was strange that when they declassified, they blocked out quite a few things.

She sometimes refers to page 72.

It is my understanding that the blackened name after Project Security Officer CIA's — was my husband. I had been told, unofficially, by a friend this was true and I know that his area of assignment and expertise was security. The agency has never acknowledged just what his individual role was. In their defense, I never prodded. My husband and I met when we both worked for the FBI and I had learned over the years not to question too much.[18]

Today, she believes her husband was the head of security, but she doesn't know what he would have been doing in that position on the project.

People who have spent their whole lives burying their frustrations from years of unanswered questions and then suddenly having to dig them back up again suffer a range of emotions. The family of William Marr was no different. Reading the declassified details of the accident today brings "a great swell of grief and tears," to his son who was only nine at the time.

He cared greatly for his family and his job. He would have done anything for either, and did.[19]

William Marr died believing he only had two children —but a third child was on the way. Sidney was pregnant at the time.[20]

Decades later, the daughter he never knew, Jan Larish, visited Las Vegas with her husband. She looked toward the mountains and thought about the sad day she lost her father.

How horrible to think that there is still debris scattered about.[21]

Terence J. O'Donnell

Occupation: Security
Employer: CIA
DOB: September 16, 1933
Age: 22
Marital status: Single

Courtesy of O'Donnell family

There is no mystery behind what it took to become a CIA agent in the 1940s; just talk to Terence O'Donnell's mother.

"I am hard of hearing, but we will put in a little attachment," Terrence's 94-year-old mother said as she delicately placed her hearing aid and prepared to talk about her son.

She reached into the depths of her memory that covers nearly a century, and pulled out thoughts of the young man that made her so proud regardless of his mysterious work. It still isn't clear to her what exactly he was doing for the CIA, so the proudest moments are the ones she saw for herself.

"My son was a very fine young man. He knew how to swim," she said and then realized how modest she was being.

At a very young age living in the Bronx, he got a job working for the health spa and they had a swimming pool and he went there to teach swimming. At a young age he was teaching swimming in our neighborhood. He got a group together to swim and trained them and then eventually, in time, they entered into a contest and they won in swimming.

By getting the swimming group together, Terrence filled a void in the urban community, a sure sign that he was capable of something greater as a leader and a performer. That was early on in high school.

He was born in the Borough of Manhattan, in New York City, and could have been just another kid from the Bronx on Teller Avenue. He went to the All Hollows Grammar School near Joyce Kilmer Park and later lived in the working class neighborhood of Parkchester inside the Bronx, sharing the streets with people of all ethnicities and religions. In 1940, Parkchester was ten square blocks of high-rise apartment buildings inhabited by twelve thousand families. It was a self-contained community and his mother admired the accessibility of bus and subway lines. The average household in Parkchester was headed by a working father with a mother fully occupied raising their children. Terrence's family was no different. Like so many there, he was the descendant of immigrants. He was named after his grandfather, Terence O'Donnell, who immigrated from Tipperary County, Ireland.

From 1941 to 1947, he attended St. Raymond's Elementary School with his six brothers and sisters. Then he went on to Cardinal Hayes High School, an all-boys school in the Bronx. It was not far from Yankee Stadium, and about a half-hour subway ride from Parkchester. The Cardinal Hayes High School motto was, and still is, "For God and Country," a motto Terrence seemed to wear like a badge throughout his work.

During his high school and college years, he went to dances, parties, football and basketball games, and proms. He marched with his classmates in the annual St. Patrick's Day Parade up New York's Fifth Avenue. Cardinal Hayes is also where Terrence began to shine, especially when he was near a glistening body of water.

He loved sports and was an exceptionally talented swimmer. He joined the Swimming Team and spent much of the fall and winter months practicing and participating in swim meets. He went on to set school records and win many interscholastic medals throughout his four years at Hayes.

As a student there, "Terry" matured physically and mentally. He learned about life, and about God and Country, his family remembers. He also seemed to hone his natural leadership and interpersonal skills. As an athlete, Terry learned self-discipline and perseverance.

He was elected Captain of the Swimming Team in his senior year in high school and won a scholarship to Fordham University because of his swimming ability.

At Fordham, Terry was a "day hopper," commuting daily by bus between his home in Parkchester and the Fordham Rose Hill Campus, about a half-hour away. That's also where he joined the Army Reserve Officers Training Corps (ROTC).

Under the direction of the Fordham Swimming Coach, John Lyttle, Terry won eleven meets over fourteen outings in his senior year alone. In that same year (1954–55), Terry was elected Captain, as well as "Most Valuable" member of his college Swimming Team.

The badges of accomplishments just kept piling up. He completed the American National Red Cross Swimming and New York City Lifeguard training courses. He donated blood and volunteered as a Swimming Instructor for the Westchester-Bronx Branch of the Young Men's Christian Association (YMCA).

From 1949 to 1954, he also used his skills working for the City of New York as a lifeguard at Orchard Beach in the Bronx. During the summer, thousands of New Yorkers thronged to the waters of Orchard Beach. The great swimmer that he was, Terry saved the lives of many potential drowning victims and rendered first aid to many others during those summers. His leadership, maturity, and heroism were recognized time and again, and led

Terry to be promoted to the position of Lieutenant of the fifty-man lifeguard staff.

Terry's faith was put to the test during his senior year at Fordham in 1954. In September of that year, his youngest brother, six-year-old John, contracted polio and died a month later. Terry's brother, Tom, recalls how Terry dealt with the tragedy.

Terry accepted God's permissive will in the death of John, believing that God had taken him home to Heaven. Terry resolved to stay close to John by staying close to God, and achieved this through frequent attendance at Mass and reception of Holy Eucharist.

In 1954 Terry was in high demand. He had always enjoyed working with young people. The Christian Brothers wanted him to become a teacher at the private school. The New York City Board of Education also wanted to hire Terry as a swimming teacher, and made him a job offer on May 24, 1955. But he knew that on graduation day, June 8, 1955, he would be commissioned as a Second Lieutenant in the Army Reserve. This, in turn, meant he would have to go on active duty with the Army for two years.

His brother Tom said,

It was no surprise why Terry O'Donnell's name was submitted to the CIA recruiter who came to Fordham in early 1955. The faculty members who recommended Terry knew he was a mature, loyal, intelligent, talented and virtuous person, who could be trusted to protect and defend the United States and its secrets.

When the CIA offered him the job, he discussed the offer with his parents.

"They were looking for twelve young men," his mother Grace remembered. They had a "particular job" in mind, she said. That's all Terry told her. "We were very proud that he was picked."

Little did she know, her son would essentially be taken off the map, entering a netherworld, obscured by secrets, a culture of classified government projects to which even a son's mother is not privy.

We used to write to him but we never wrote to him in his own name. I don't remember the name of the man we put on the letter, but he [Terrence] would always get it. I didn't question it because I was an obedient citizen.

By 1955, they didn't even know that Terry's CIA work had taken him to the Los Angeles area. Letters to and from Terry were sent through a third party. In a letter dated September 5, 1955, Terry wrote to his then eight-year-old sister, Jo, to commend her for becoming a good swimmer.

Jo, I bet you didn't know that I flew in one of those big planes you see in the sky. Yes, I am going to many interesting places and always by airplane.

No matter where he had been, he made it to the O'Donnell family summer vacation at Trout Lake, near Lake George, in New York's Adirondack Mountains. He took one last break from his secret life to swim and fish in the clean, cool water of that lovely lake. He also climbed nearby Cat Mountain, and joined in on the hayrides and the square dances. Always the big brother and coach, he used his time at Trout Lake to give individual swimming lessons to his sisters and brothers, whether they wanted them or not. Then he went back to work. Not long after his last vacation, the son Grace O'Donnell treasured was gone.

Tom remembers that the family and friends of Terry O'Donnell were heartbroken and in a state of shock. The first notice of the accident, Tom says, came in a late night phone call from the CIA to Terry's dad. Terry's sister Grace ran immediately to the St. Raymond's Rectory and returned with Father Dan Shea, who prayed with them and attempted to console Terry's mom and dad.

But Grace recalls a different way she was notified.

We got a knock on the door one night and it was a gentleman coming in to tell us that our son had been in an accident.

In the world of mysteries that had surrounded her son, one thing was for sure: how he died.

From what we had known and my impression was that it (the accident) was an airplane, because if it was a boat, he could have swum to shore.

Word of his death spread pretty fast through the groups of young men and girls he had coached.

In college, Terry had also been an officer in the Holy Name Society and the Moderator and Coach of the parish Catholic Youth Organization (CYO) Swimming Team, which won a Bronx County Championship. In June 2001, Tony Bruno, a retired civil servant, recalled having been coached by Terry. Bruno said,

Terry will always be remembered by all of us folks that swam on his teams. He was an outstanding person who gave his all to help the youth in his time. I personally would have loved to tell him how much I have learned from him.

One of his Cardinal Hayes classmates, Terence P. Curran, PhD, now a Professor at Siena College, remembered Terry in May 2001 as:

A star athlete on the swim team and a very nice guy. I remember my shock at hearing of his death in an airplane crash.

Several days after the accident, a CIA escort officer delivered Terry's body in a sealed casket to New York's Penn Station. The escort officer also handed his family a small cloth bag containing Terry's Fordham class ring and his Miraculous Medal, both of which Terry was wearing at the time of his death.

His funeral was held at St. Raymond's Church on November 28th. Father Shea conducted the Funeral Mass attended by hundreds of Terry's friends, neighbors, teachers, priests, and swim team and family members.

As Terry's flag-draped casket was led from the church to the hearse, he received one last tribute from his friends and swim team members, who formed an Honor Guard along the church walkway.

He was laid to rest in the Gate of Heaven Cemetery, next to the remains of his brother John and his Grandpa O'Donnell. When the graveside service came to an end, the flag of a grateful nation that had been placed on his casket was presented to Terry's parents. Today, most people who visit that cemetery go to see a very different hero, Babe Ruth. Little do they know the quiet remembrance of another more obscure and dedicated hero, Terence O'Donnell, is right nearby.

Among the visitors to his grave is one of Terry's other sisters, Johanna O'Donnell-Gross, who was too young to remember the day he died. She can put the years following his death into perspective even though she only has two memories of her brother. One is very ordinary — going to his high school graduation. The other memory is of the day he died.

Being seven [years old] there was a tremendous void in the family. My mother was one of ten children and I remember all the aunts and uncles gathering in our home when they knew that Terry had died. There were many, many people in our apartment and trying to console our parents as best they could.

Today, she doesn't resent Terry's sacrifice.

My brother believed that he was being a patriot.

While Terry's sister was content simply knowing that her brother was the ultimate patriot, the impact on Terry's mother was much more painful and difficult to understand. Grace O'Donnell painfully remembered:

I almost went out of my mind to begin with and it was a good thing that I had a good husband who could take over and listen and we lived through that terrible tragedy which was the worse thing that happened to me in my life. At the time I believe it was a government secret. Do you know, when I found out what he was involved in 43 years later, the government called me up and invited me to Washington. My husband didn't even live to see that day.

Grace's husband passed away in 1984. By that time, the truth of his son's death and mission had sat in a file gathering dust for twenty-nine years. Nine years later, in September 1998, Grace got an unexpected invitation in the mail. It was the announcement of the declassification ceremony of the U-2. And for the first time they knew the "fact that the November 17, 1955 crash on Mount Charleston was linked to the U-2 project"[22] and her son.

But they still didn't know how he was involved, how he died, or why until the Silent Heroes of the Cold War contacted them. Even though it was decades later, part of real closure was returning to the mountain. Tom recalled the day he brought their mom to see the crash site.

We took grandma to the 7,000 foot level of Mount Charleston from which point she could see the site of the November 17, 1955 plane crash. This was the first time Grandma had been to the place of dread and sorrow. She now understands why in the cold and snow of November 1955, it took the recovery team several days to get to the crash site.

There she was brought together with her son's friends that she never knew existed, people like Jim Byrne who had a different knowledge of her son. Jim told her about Terry's work at "The Ranch," which was the name some of them used for the U-2 test site. Byrne, who was also a CIA Security Officer at the time, said that while at "The Ranch," they lived in barracks, two to a room, and that Terry was his roommate. Byrne described Terry as an "ideal roommate, very pleasant, happy, and seemed to be always working out, keeping in shape. He was very religious."

Byrne pointed out that there were no religious services at "The Ranch," but on periodic work breaks back in the Burbank, California area, Terry would attend Mass. He considers Terry to be a hero and to be one of the nicest persons he had the honor of knowing.

As a personal tribute, there on that high mountain Byrne presented Terry's mother with a CIA medallion.

Grandma, of course, was brought to tears as were a few others. This unplanned event seemed so appropriate to me, for Grandma had clearly overcome her dread of the place; and despite her sorrows, her age, and physical infirmities, she boldly went to see where her Terry had died. In doing so, she met some of the other people for whom November 17, 1955, was a life-changing date and who also suffered just as she had suffered.[23]

Since Terry was thought of as such an excellent role model, Fordham University honored him by creating The Terrence J. O'Donnell Memorial Award, which is today presented to the Fordham athlete who best exemplifies the qualities of sportsmanship, loyalty, dedication, and self-discipline.

Courtesy of Pappas family

George Manual Pappas, Jr.

Occupation: Pilot, 1st Lieutenant
Employer: United States Air Force
DOB: August 9, 1928
Age: 27
Marital status: Married

The passengers on November 17, 1955, were literally in distinguished hands. Pilot George Manuel Pappas held the Air Medal with its two oak leaf clusters and had also been awarded the Distinguished Flying Cross in 1954.

"When my mother died and grandmother died, I pulled out all of his pictures and dog tags. I have all his stuff. I am just sitting here looking at it," says Jo-Lynne, Pappas' niece. She does sit a lot, surrounded by a pile of what's left of his belongings. She goes over the few memories she has, trying to build a personality around the man based on these trinkets. She was only six years old when he died.

I remember being little. He was all over the world. When I look through all the stuff, I don't know what to think. My mother and grandmother and grandfather are deceased, so the people who really knew him are gone.

Jo-Lynne looks at his Florida driver's license which shows he was of average build at 5 foot 9 inches and about 160 pounds; he had brown eyes and black hair.

He was a handsome, good-looking guy. He was smart and he did a good job. He was a good pilot and got picked to go to all sorts of places.

Pappas was the one person who knew the exact location of the secret government airbase. He could pinpoint it on a map and fly to the new secret airbase virtually blind every day, and did. The location was something he never shared, not even to his closest relatives. Jo-Lynne remembered:

My mother had just been down to visit him the month before. He couldn't tell her anything. Everything he did was top-secret. Back then with the Russians and stuff, there was a lot of speculation.

The Pappas family never knew where he was until the day he died, when what was left of his body lay in the frozen gravel above 11,000 feet at Mount Charleston.

My mother is his sister and she got a phone call. My grandmother and grandfather went to San Antonio to get his body. They [Air Force] said no need to go to Las Vegas because they couldn't do anything there.

Among the things that Jo-Lynne has left to remember him by is a letter from Major Bullock of the 76th Air Transport Squadron, written to George's wife after the crash.

Pappas had been selected for promotion but unfortunately his death occurred before the action could be completed.

The letter meant that he was posthumously promoted to Captain, but the letter dated December 13, 1955, was also a disappointment:

No increased pay or gratuities may be derived from such action. I share your pride in your husband's exemplary performance of duty.[24]

Another letter to Florence Summers, Pappas' mother was light on details, but also commended him.

"His likeable personality was compounded with intelligence, common sense, and outstanding ability as an aviator," Major Bullock wrote. He also told her something that was not in the accident report. That at 8:05 a.m. on November 17, Pappas made contact with Nellis

Air Force Base, "having visual reference to the terrain and was cleared to his destination under visual flight rules."[25] They now know that was not true.

However, the family did have some real facts they could hold onto as they weathered a storm of criticism being the family of the pilot. Pappas, like all pilots, need what's called an "instrument certificate" in order to fly in conditions when visibility is low. According to the documents Jo-Lynne has, Pappas' certificate was current and not set to expire until August 9, 1956, another nine months.

In spite of being a distinguished and qualified airman, he was raised to keep his family in mind while on his many secret missions. Jo-Lynne recalled:

He would always come and surprise me. He had gone somewhere in the Pacific Islands and brought me back a hula skirt. I have a picture of him hanging up now.

Today Jo-Lynne still gets tears in her eyes when she looks at that black and white picture for too long. It reminds her of the intense and long-term pain her family endured.

My uncle, being the pilot, people [the families of other victims] would look at him as being responsible.

She wasn't exaggerating. With the facts obscured by a veil of secrecy, many blamed the pilot for lack of anyone else to blame. In fact, in one of Steve Ririe's early conversations with a family member, after seeing Pappas named as the pilot, said, "That's the man who killed my father," Ririe recalled. That statement alone sent shivers through Ririe, keeping him awake at night, wondering if it really was the pilot's fault. That kind of comment inspired Ririe to embark on the seemingly impossible mission of finding out what happened, for the sake of the people whom he never even knew.

There was something very unsettling surrounding the

case of George Pappas and his family. That may be why he appeared in Julie Ririe's dream, if it was him, while she and her family were camping in 1999 at the base of the crash site. Pappas' family suffered immensely from the secrecy.

Like everybody would think that he wasn't capable. It was his error or something and it was him and a co-pilot and a navigator. I can imagine that people thought it was pilot error when indeed it wasn't, Jo-Lynne said.

Some would never know the truth and others wouldn't find out until it almost didn't matter anymore.

It was locked up, closed, top-secret and locked up. It wasn't talked about, there wasn't anything to say; nobody said anything. Nobody did anything.

But Jo-Lynne managed to keep faith. Despite the pressure from the military and the other families, she still wants to talk about it and express relief that Pappas did his best to save the precious lives of the men on this secret project.

My grandmother never got over it [his death]. They never had closure. All the good things that he [George] was trying to do for our country. As far as him radioing for help and them [the airbase] not letting him know where he was. They never knew that.

The sense of Jo-Lynne's relief can only heal to the extent that her parents and grandparents were denied closure.

I am probably the one with the least information and the only one left to speak on his behalf. I know it is devastating to not know why in hell.

Pappas' parents and family didn't live to know the truth. The only way Jo-Lynne can describe it today is by using the same word, "terrible," over and over to describe the feelings over the last five decades of her life.

When she finally saw the records, she wished her mother, grandmother, and grandfather were still alive to see that it wasn't his fault, that the conclusion should not be pilot error.

I think they should tell the families as much as they can without breaching the secrets. They should tell them they are working on something that is top-secret. He and the co-pilot are the only ones who were being looked at as responsible.

She says she understands that he worked for the government, he signed up for the job, and it was top-secret.

"I do. Again, there was a protocol." While the protocol was secrecy, it's ironic that crash documents show there was a lack of protocol, a lack of adherence to existing Air Force protocol that, in fact, may have contributed to his death. Even while Jo-Lynne believes the military did the best they could to follow protocol, she says they didn't do enough in the follow-up to the accident.

I do think they owe something to the family, to put some sort of conclusion on their part as to what, why, and how.

She says the military should have made more of an effort to find the families, too. Finding out through a stranger made her feelings toward the military even worse. Fortunately, she says Pappas didn't have any children. She says she can't imagine what his wife was told, that she would just never see him again.

Pappas was married to a young lady named JoAnn. She remarried after the accident. All the pictures of her and Pappas were destroyed in a fire in 2001. Steve Ririe did contact Pappas' widow, but she didn't want to talk about it.

While the widow JoAnn has moved on, Jo-Lynne has refused to let go of the terrible tragedy that has cost her family so much. She has always kept alive the memory of her Uncle George.

Today, Jo-Lynne says JoAnn prefers to forget because all that is left was the blame others had for Pappas, she says.

"I wish she (JoAnn) would tell me some stories," Jo-Lynne says staring at his picture on her wall.

And if JoAnn did choose to delve back into those memories of the past and share them, Jo-Lynne's son might have one more role model to live by.

It is a tragic situation. I am sorry, but I don't know him [George]. I didn't get a chance to.

But she keeps that black and white portrait of him up on the wall, and sometimes she turns to her son:

I tell my son, I think you look a lot like my uncle George.

<hr />

The trip to the top of the mountain for the victims organized by the Silent Heroes of the Cold War held special meaning for what was left of the Pappas family. The night before this journey, the families of the victims attended a greeting dinner at the home of Dwayne and Judy Brown. As they pulled up chairs around a table together for the first time, there was something very uncomfortable in the air.

Steve Ririe felt the tension. Rolling around in the back of his mind was a fear that someone at the dinner table would start to blame Pappas and other flight crew, comments he worried would be devastating, sending his entire effort backward into a path of pain and regenerating the silence. His plan was to try to keep the families focused on the memorial. The dinner started with State Senator Ray Rawson giving a presentation to them about the effort to get Congress to designate a national memorial. His presentation included a timeline of the accident and almost immediately, someone in the group inter-rupted with the very question Steve feared. The families looked across the table toward each other.

"It was pretty tense," Steve recalled.

It was the kind of tense moment that could either turn a group into a lynch mob or one that would move them together to consensus in an effort to avoid the mistakes of the past.

All the families quickly chimed in. To my joy and relief, the families quickly affirmed their support for the Pappas and Winham families. I knew immediately everything would be okay from that moment. I knew that the project to build a memorial to the men of USAF 9068 had nothing to do with blame and everything to do with honoring the unsung heroes that deserve our nation's gratitude.

Harold C. Silent

Occupation: Physicist
Employer: Hycon Manufacturing Company
DOB: September 26, 1896
Age: 59
Marital status: Married

Courtesy of Denny Thatcher

At 59 years old, Harold Silent had decades more experience than anyone else on the flight. He had already seen a number of secret government projects as one of the many great minds working behind the scenes. There was one way to know he was a genius: "Just in working with him," one of his colleagues at Hycon Manufacturing, Denny Thatcher remembered.

He would always come up with the answers that the management of our company would ask. He was one of the top consultants.

Thatcher worked with him first as an electronics technician back in 1949. His first project with Silent was to construct what he called "a large rack and panel design of electronics, which would house the central controls for a US Navy system."

Silent was one of the finest gentlemen I have ever known, and possibly the most intelligent. We worked well together.

As a physicist, there was little Silent couldn't work on, from voice-operated switching devices on the first commercial trans-Atlantic telephone to spending several years in Hollywood with the advent of sound in movies, called the "talkies." He also worked in Norway on a patent case and departed just thirty hours before the Germans invaded in World War II, according to his obituary.

During the war, he was on the staff of the National Defense Research Council at Duke University, improving artillery detection and acoustical range-finding equipment. His work as a consultant for several branches of the military took him all over the world. Thatcher was able to gather that a few of the places Silent went to were Guam, the Arizona and Nevada deserts, and many classified ocean voyages. Silent didn't talk about his projects, so the projects Thatcher worked on with Silent were the only ones he knew about.

I wasn't really privy to a lot of that. He came up with one way of doing something at the Salton Sea. They wanted to get all of these 35-millimeter cameras to aim them at torpedoes.

The goal in that project was to fire torpedoes from one end of the Salton Sea to the other and have cameras triggered to take pictures of them as they flew.

Torpedoes were launched at the southern end of the Salton Sea; we had 35 millimeters cameras set all over the range and the idea was to get all of these so that we would know where we were in terms of the launching point and know exactly where they were within milliseconds. They would cover several miles of distance every second across the Salton Sea.

He and Silent did prove the feasibility, but the project was never completed.

They called him "Si" — "Si" Silent; he was always silent.

The fact that he was a man of few words made him all around mysterious. "Yes, very (mysterious)," Thatcher remembers. "Out at lunch time he was always with management. We never saw him out with anyone."

One of Thatcher's projects with Silent was the Hycon Model "B" camera. He said:

They [the government or CIA] kept giving us briefings,

not divulging any of the information they would come up with.

"We had something called the "B" configuration camera," Thatcher remembered. Used in the U-2, it had a tremendous capability to hold film, he said. After the film was exposed, it could be pulled into a magazine and held. But in order to do that, the film needed to be only a few thousandths of an inch thick. That capability of holding a lot of film meant it could take pictures all across Europe.

The camera Silent worked on became the world's premier high-resolution, high-altitude camera that enabled the United States to conduct routine reconnaissance in relative safety and to observe global hot spots in astonishing detail while putting very few lives at risk. It was this camera that provided proof of the existence of Soviet missiles in Cuba in 1962.

At the time the plane itself was pretty remarkable. "It was extremely wide film and they had a plane load of it when they took off," he remembered. He and Silent watched a few of the U-2s take off at Area 51, too. They were part of a small group of Hycon employees who were there from the beginning.

I was up there on the day that they first flew the U-2.

He says it was a very strange time.

Yeah, it was, I didn't know where I was, I had never heard of Watertown and Site [Area] 51. A lot of things went on out there and we never dared tell anyone where we were going.

Part of keeping this level of secrecy wasn't complicated at all. The CIA went straight for the men's stomachs — the stomach being one way to a man's heart; a happy stomach is also less likely to grumble.

We ate very, very well; we had good places to stay. The food couldn't have been better. I am sure that we ate

*steak too often. We had lobster and a lot of gourmet
type dishes.*

Maybe a better name for Area 51 would have been
Mouthwatering town. In any case, Thatcher says he
had just gotten off the plane in Watertown one morning when it left again to get more employees, including
Silent and Hanks.

*The way that it happened was a perfectly normal op-
eration. That is how I went for many, many days in
a row until we got trailers out there and then I lived
out there.*

Though the secrecy has long since vanished, "I haven't
been debriefed to this point," Thatcher says, adding that
he assumes it's probably okay to talk about this now.
He wasn't ever told what the consequences would be of
talking about Watertown and the work there.

*They kept coming around saying, 'thou shalt not say
this, this, and this.' A lot of us who were involved in
the U-2 have never been able to talk about it. And they
never really came out and said 'Yeah, you can talk
about this,' and so some of this is still under wraps.*

Other than his remarkable work, there was nothing
that made Silent stand out.

*He was very gentlemanly, because working with all
the engineers at Hycon; he was always a gentleman.
They loved him because he was a gentleman, he was
that first [a gentleman] and then he was a man of so
much intelligence, because we were stunned when
he would come up with something and the way he
would respond. He could work well with just about
anybody. He had a wife that I never met. He would
make reference to her in a nice manner. Being the
very gentlemanly man that he was, I never heard him
use profanity.*

The Silent Heroes of the Cold War could not locate any

immediate family of Harold Silent other than a cousin who lives in Houston, Texas.

The end of his life was only marked by a brief obituary in the *Los Angeles Times* of Nov. 23, 1955:

> *Private funeral services were held for Harold C. Silent, 59, physicist who lost his life Nov. 17 in the Air Force C-54 that crashed atop Mount Charleston near Las Vegas.*
>
> *Mr. Silent was acting as a consultant on research with the Defense Department at the time of the crash. The plane was en route from Norton AFB to the Nevada Atomic Bombing range when it struck the mountain.*
>
> *During World War II, Mr. Silent was associated with the National Defense Research Council at Duke University, devoting his time to research and development of military weapons.*

Thatcher also explained that, since the war, Silent went on to serve as a consultant for various military groups and for the Hycon Manufacturing Company of Pasadena.[26]

> *Harold Charles Silent was born Sept. 26, 1896 in Azusa, California from an old family of Glendora, California. He was educated at Cornell University and was a talented physicist.*

His accomplishment speaks in silence.

Courtesy of Urolatis family

Edwin J. Urolatis

Occupation: Security
Employer: CIA
DOB: June 8, 1928
Age: 27
Marital status: Married

Edwin Urolatis did not have an easy upbringing in Brockton, Massachusetts. His family was steeped in tradition that was designed for survival in a world where work was hard to come by and family was all you had.

Oh yeah, we came from a poor immigrant Polish family. My grandparents barely spoke English till the day they died, Edwin's niece, Marcia Urolatis Charter, remembers.

Back then there was a general lack of respect for immigrants and Marcia remembers the way school children treated them.

I don't know if they thought that there was something different about us, but the kids in the neighborhood used to call us 'The Communists.' A kid named Sean would get on the bus in front of me and he would kick me and say 'I am kicking the Communists.'

Edwin, however, strived to rise above that, with a keen desire for acceptance. He worked at becoming a star in the tiny world of Brockton.

Edwin was the prize. He played basketball. He was tall, thin, and he was the big basketball star.

But like many of the victims of the mountain crash, most of the stories of his personality as a child are lost today.

I remember he carried me around on his shoulders all

*the time. He was tall and I was little. My mother would
have the stories or my father would have the stories,
but they are gone.*

Though little is known about his personal and professional life, a few years after the crash documents were released, *The Sunday Enterprise* in Brockton began the task of trying to rebuild the pieces of Edwin's life. Through the paper's account it's easy to ascertain that, if he was oppressed by a society that was hard on immigrants at the time, Edwin Urolatis didn't hold it against anyone. He found his own way to prove people wrong, and combat their critical eye. He did it by finding a place where he could shine and perform for the people who made life difficult for him and his family.

"The Brockton man was extremely well liked by all who knew him," the Brockton reporter wrote. "He was of a quiet, unassuming nature except when on the basketball court. The antics coupled with his expert play provided hilarious moments for fans of Brockton High School and Brown University."[27]

School records showed Edwin was a guard on the junior varsity high school team. His coach, Arthur E. Staff, remembered that a year before his graduation, he would spend nearly every Sunday for several hours at the YMCA trying to perfect his shot.

It worked. In the following season, the coach shifted him to center because of his expert shooting ability, especially his ability with one-handed (hook) shots. That year, the team reached the "Tech tourney" championship semi-finals.

In that tournament, the team was playing the New Bedford High Whalers. As the game neared its end, Edwin's team was just one point behind. The retired basketball coach of Brockton High School recalled that Edwin was the key in the last few seconds of the game. He had been fouled and was awarded two free-throw shots that could have tied, or even won the game. But as he stepped up to the free through line, his coach watched as Edwin, in his focus and desire to win, dropped his signature one-handed shot for the more conventional two-handed shot.

In those days a coach wasn't allowed to yell orders from the sidelines and the coach could only watch nervously as Edwin prepared for a two-handed shot. Both shots missed and Edwin left the floor brokenhearted, his team defeated 34–33. The coach said that Edwin gave the best team a run for its money; the Whalers went on to win the tournament championship.

He was one of the greatest players, sportsmen, and gentlemen that I ever coached, the coach declared.

Edwin graduated that year in 1946 and joined the Navy. Two years later he was discharged as an electronic Technician's Mate Third Class and went to Brown University. There he majored in Russian history and played basketball. In 1950 he graduated and studied for two years at Columbia University toward a doctorate in the liberal arts college.

"He was very quiet, very quiet and he was sort of a professional scholar," his sister-in-law Barbara Urolatis remembers. *"He went to Russia and studied there. He was very intelligent, but he was not boisterous. He wouldn't let you know at all what he knew."*

While somewhere inside of this man was that excitement from high school, his reputation for intelligence was passed down through the generations.

"He went around from college to college," his nephew Alan Urolatis recalled.

He was very knowledgeable. Both he and my father knew like eight languages. My father was an interpreter. Coming from Poland you had to know at least three languages because the border would change so often.

When he came back from the University, his family found that he was doing something different.

"When he came back, he was working for Proctor and Gamble with the job of selling chemical supplies or soap," Marcia remembered what they were told. That didn't seem strange to her at the time, but for others in the family who look back now, his nephew Alan sees the story didn't make much sense.

Officially, he was working for Proctor and Gamble and that's all we knew for years. Sales? That is a little far-fetched for a professional student.

Late one night on November 17, 1955, Alan remembers that his parents got a phone call.

I was jumping on the back of the couch. I was five, I was little. My father said, 'No, it can't be him, he works for Proctor and Gamble. It can't be him.' I remember how my father denied it.

Alan's parents refused to give up hope and went back to work as usual in the morning. His father went back to work at the "gang room" at the John E. Foote Company factory and his mother at the London Clothing Company factory.

Somehow they got a report, possibly generated by speculation in the shroud of secrecy, that a "snow jeep" was dropped at the wreckage by a rescue team and that the plane was headed for a super secret Atomic Energy Commission installation carrying atomic scientists and civilians.

When the bodies were recovered, federal agents did talk to Edwin's father directly, but for some reason they only told him that his son was a salesman.

That was the story that everyone gave us. To the day my father died, he didn't know what his son did.

The pain of burying Edwin was prolonged for his family compared to other victims. At 10:15 one morning, Edwin's mother and father went to the Boston train station to wait for his closed-casket body to arrive on the Boston–New York Owl Express. But they waited and waited with no train until an abrupt announcement declared that the passengers would not be arriving. The train had derailed in Norwalk, Connecticut. The mourning family went home. They probably retained some hope that he was somehow still alive on that train, but after the derailment, he surely was dead.

"Everyone used to say Uncle Eddie died twice," David Urolatis, Edwin's nephew recalled to *The Sunday Enterprise.*[28]

Eventually his body did arrive and unlike the other sealed and closed caskets, his father had to identify the body. Barbara Urolatis recalls what he saw:

From what I understand, when they saw him he was dismembered and he was all swollen. And whether he had gained a great deal of weight before this crash we don't know, but it certainly didn't look like him. He was very tall and slender, but the body that came home was puffed up. It didn't appear to be the same man, but it was him. They recognized him and everything about his body was in really rough shape.

She says the military did not handle this well at all. The family was never told that he was anything other than a salesman, a salesman who somehow died on a remote mountain top in the middle of the desert and whose body was mangled almost beyond recognition. The newspapers and radio said for some reason he was on that plane with atomic scientists to a super secret airbase. For this immigrant family that had fled a Cold War zone of turmoil and secrets, it must have seemed as if the government or someone had kidnapped or tortured him. This was exactly the kind of situation his parents had probably hoped to leave behind. The kind of situation they had hoped to protect their children from by coming to America.

We were back in the Cold War then, but definitely they could have told us. We could have been proud that he was involved in a government project. We could have known that there were other people on the plane that we could have talked to. They [the government] could have let us know what was going on. It would have given us closure.

Instead, there was an open wound that bled through the generations.

My father became an alcoholic and had a nervous breakdown. It was a very tight family; they worked for the coat factory and the fact that one of them would go off and do something different was unfathomable.

She partially blames the secrecy for her family's problems on her father's early death.

Did it cause it? No. Did it contribute to it? Yes, but did it cause it? No.

Edwin's father died in 1961, his mother in 1991, and his brother died a year later.

They were buried next to Edwin whose headstone is engraved with the only information they ever knew:

EDWIN J. KILLED IN PLANE CRASH LAS VEGAS NEVADA, THEIR SON.

Courtesy of Winham family

Paul Eugene Winham

Occupation: Co-pilot
Employer: United States Air Force
DOB: June 4, 1931
Age: 24
Marital status: Married

Paul "Gene" Winham had a blessed and simple upbringing on a Dexter, New Mexico farm with his brother, Troy.

We worked on the farm and went swimming in the afternoons, Troy said.

That's where the family grew cotton, alfalfa, and grain. Paul was seven years older than Troy. He still remembers that his brother was really good with the farm machinery. He would come back from school in the summers and help out on the farm.

He was just all around handy at anything he done. Whether it was books or machinery, or anything like that.

He was good with his hands and his mind, as well as being good looking. He was also voted best dressed in school.

He was good at anything he ever done; very intelligent and athletic. Anything he ever attempted he was real good at it, Troy said.

Paul had the record to prove it. He graduated early from high school at age sixteen; he was the valedictorian and was in ROTC. He had scholarship offers to several universities, including the Colorado School of Mines. But he went to Oklahoma State University and graduated with a degree in business administration.

What Paul really loved was flying and through the Air Force ROTC, he was able to join the Air Force where he specialized in multi-engine aircraft.

From what we could gather, he was considered one of the top pilots in his division, which was probably why he was picked for this mission, Troy said.

He went to flight training in Columbus, Mississippi and graduated from Reese Air Force Base flight school on April 14, 1954. He was assigned to Kelly Air Force Base in Texas on May 1st and left home on November 14, 1954. What's odd is that he left without telling his family where else he might be going.[29]

Just three days shy of a year later, Troy was sitting in front of the TV in New Mexico when a big story came across the tube.

We saw the [story of the] crash on TV and we saw the guards guarding it but we had no idea he was on board it. Or what he was doing. It just said they weren't aware of what they were doing, but it must have been some kind of top-secret mission. They showed us the crash picture, where the wreckage had mushroomed.

It didn't occur to him that his brother could be on board. The last time Troy had heard from Paul was in Paul's senior year.

He called and I was about to graduate and he called and congratulated me. We knew he was on top-secret work. We just didn't know where he was and his wife didn't even know where he was. He was just gone.

So that crash on TV was just some mysterious accident and at the time it meant virtually nothing to this young man. It meant nothing more than it would to any citizen who happened to be watching TV that day.

It was just kind of unknown. The news people said it had to be something important because of the guards and the quietness around it and they wouldn't let them get close to it and we didn't know "Gene" was onboard or even where he was.

So they went on with their normal lives believing Troy was out there flying somewhere. But those were the last few normal days before two Air Force representatives, including a Colonel, showed up at their door on the farm.

At first we were told he was missing and they didn't know if there were any survivors and it was several days later when they contacted us and told us he had lost his life. I was in shock.

The Colonel offered only one vague consolation.

They said, 'Some day you will be proud to know he was part of it.' We were never contacted again.

After the Colonel left, the family was distraught and alone. Troy remembers his parents trying to cope with the loss, but having little to fill the void that was left. He watched in the following days as his parents rummaged through Paul's belongings, searching for some answers, some clue as to what happened and why, or anything that would tell them what he was doing. But no answers emerged.

Not a whole lot, just pictures and memories of that nature.

The only concrete truth they knew was that they had lost a precious son. They waited day in and day out for that news the Colonel had said would come and make them so proud, the news that would make their son a hero. What they got instead was a rumor from Troy's cousin, who was also in the Air Force. That cousin told the family what he had been told, that Paul was at the yoke at the time of the crash and was responsible for the fourteen deaths. They believed it; what other choice did they have?

My brother Paul was at the controls of the plane when it went down and that the Captain was at the back of the plane when it went down. And we actually thought that for many years.[30]

To be exact, they believed that rumor for forty-eight years. What they didn't know is that the true answer was sitting in a top-secret document that no one ever evaluated to determine who was flying the plane. The years they spent searching for clues and asking for answers from the Air Force must have felt like being a mime in a glass box; no one seemed to hear them as they ran up against an invisible wall.

"They couldn't figure out why it went down." But they did gather some tidbits of information, such as the fact that the flight was given visual clearance and that they were crossing an area they weren't really supposed to be. "For many years that is all we heard," Troy recalled.

Steve Winham, Paul's youngest brother, was only ten years old at the time of the accident. Somewhere along the line he also picked up the fact that the flight was on an unapproved route. Steve had to assign his own reasoning to it:

I had always thought that the pilot just made the decision to use the shorter route on his own.

This dark path of secrets that led to Paul's death was devastating for the family. It was especially difficult for Troy who idolized his brother. How could Paul be responsible? "As an older brother, he could do nothing wrong," Troy thought.

After the rumor, they started to lose interest in what would only bring more pain. The memory of the accident began to fade into history and the family chose to preserve their sanity and accept that Paul's mission would forever remain a mystery.

The Air Force wasn't very forthcoming and we just finally accepted that we would never know. They just only told us that they couldn't elaborate on what he was doing and that some day we would be proud of him.

Then one day out of the blue, this stranger named Steve Ririe called Troy to tell him the truth.

It was a big relief. Knowing that he was a top-notch pilot and the possibility that he had made a mistake was always a question in my mind and so it was a relief to know he wasn't at the controls.

Had it not been for the accident, Troy likes to imagine that his brother would still be flying.

His plans were to stay with the Air Force until retirement and then go on to private flying.

Decades of questions that had festered deep inside Troy were finally being resolved and the belief that his brother was somehow responsible for the tragedy and death on the mountain was revealed as just a cruel rumor, a sick byproduct of government secrecy. His parents would forever be victims, forgotten sufferers who went to their graves believing their son was responsible for the crash; they never knew the importance of their son's project as the Air Force had promised they would.

Troy is very polite when he considers why the government never told them the truth. He says he knows that's how the bureaucracy operates. Still, he says the right thing to do would have been to tell them before his parents died.

Well, yeah! It would have been good if they had contacted us and let us know at a later date.

Despite the questions, they never lost confidence in Paul. They kept alive the most positive memory, the one that no one could ruin and was ultimately true.

He [Paul] was just your typical kind of all-American person who was a pilot. He was very good at what he had done and had all the confidence in the world.

If the details of the report had been made public, the world could have had confidence in him, too.

Chapter VI

The Missing Passenger

One person escaped all the pain that came from this routine C-54 flight from Burbank to Area 51. He reached career heights that the other crew members, whose lives had been cut short, were just as likely to achieve. One of the youngest passengers scheduled to be on that flight, he was twenty-four-year-old Bob Murphy. Thinking back to the many trips he took on the route, he says it was a kind of direct, no-frills flight.

Bucket seats, no service. No stewards, just transportation. You could look out the windows. They had nothing to hide from us. We were cleared [by security] to a ridiculous level.

Murphy looks back fondly on life at Area 51. It was an exciting time for everyone involved. He was sent there in July 1955 as a flight test mechanic. Four days after he arrived, they put the U-2 into the Nevada airspace. Murphy remembers:

There wasn't much there. I will tell you that. Small rooms and a mess hall and three teeny little hangars. Each one held one U-2. That was it, and the guards,

Robert Murphy seen here with body bag.

Courtesy of Kyril D. Plaskon

everyone had to recognize you. Security protocol was that if they didn't recognize you, then you couldn't go in. It didn't matter how many passes you had.

The food service was casual, with big bowls of mashed potatoes and plates full of steaks that you could stab right off the platter passed among the diners, family style.

We worked extremely long hours. I would eat five meals a day and I still lost thirty pounds.

Some of them who were there didn't even know what the overall plan or their purpose was in this barren, secret, godforsaken place.

Nobody told us what we were going to do. My big bosses knew. We guessed it. But we didn't know we were going to over-fly Russia.

Murphy remembers that sometimes on those flights to Area 51 they would fly past the ominous radioactive mushroom clouds climbing overhead as the government tested atomic bombs — a reminder of the brutal tool that could be used in case the U-2 mission failed to prevent war. Murphy continued to make the flight until 1957.

There is no question that Murphy was a passenger on these regular flights, but nowhere in the crash records is Murphy interviewed or mentioned. Steve Ririe only found out that he was supposed to be on that flight through other employees at Lockheed. Maybe he wasn't included because he was the only one who would have tied the accident to the secret airbase for any prying eyes or the media. Whatever the reason, the investigators' omission of Murphy is curious given that he may have been a key player in the flight time of the doomed craft.

A few months after Murphy started making the trip to Area 51 in July 1955, he remembers boarding the plane and seeing the new pilot, George Pappas. Murphy stopped and talked to him, telling Pappas that he had once been a flight engineer on a C-54. That inspired Pappas to give him a test. He invited Murphy into the cockpit, had him sit down and said, "Let me see you synchronize the propellers." Murphy did it pretty well and the two hit it off. Pappas told him if he were ever late, he would wait for him. It was a friendly gesture with unforeseeable consequences on November 17, 1955.

Anybody who knows me, I am never late. I never take a day off, never missed a day of work.

But one night, November 16, 1955, in Burbank, Murphy was out on a date with a girl. It was a little late and he said he had to get back because he had to catch a plane in the morning. He remembers going home and setting his clock for 5:30 a.m. to make the flight.

My clock radio played for three hours before I woke up.
'Holy gosh', I said. 'What the hell happened?'

By then, little did he know, his colleagues were already dead.

Today Murphy speaks with disdain about a British author who speculated in his book, *50 Years of the U-2*, that Murphy missed the flight that day because he drank too much the night before. Murphy denies it. Regardless, by the time he woke up, Murphy knew the flight was long gone, even if Pappas did wait for him. "No problem," he thought.

I was going to catch it the next day, and when I got
out there to the airport, the plane wasn't there. And
I said 'Gee, that's funny'. On my way back I stopped
in Burbank to have breakfast and picked up the Los
Angeles Times. *It said a plane had crashed that was*
going to Nellis, but I knew where it was going. It really
shocked me.

He went back to his apartment and started to get ready to leave to go somewhere. He doesn't remember where he was going, but he does remember what happened when he was ready to leave the door.

As I opened the door a guy was getting ready to rap on
it. As far as they knew, I was dead and he blanched
white and said, 'You are supposed to be dead. They
had you on that airplane and so they sent me to tell
your mother and wife [if you have one] you are dead.'
I said flatly to their face: 'Well, I am not!'

The young Murphy closed the door when they left, forgetting about where he was going and thought about what had just happened for a minute. He decided to call his mom in New York.

I said, 'If anyone calls you and tells you I am dead, I
am not!'

The weird deal is that they checked me off as being

on board. They told the people at the test site that I was
among the guys in the wreck.

If the crash had happened on a Monday he says it would
have wiped out the whole program:

The test pilots, the flight test management, the flight test
worker, the total organization that was at Area 51, to
support that operation.

After the accident Murphy went on to become a flight
supervisor for the test shop at Area 51, training the
crews that would operate the U-2 out of Japan.

Since Murphy didn't die on that flight, his life can be
summed up in a single word, a word the victims and
their families will never be able use to describe their
own:

Terrific. I ended up the Director of Operations of Skunk
Works [Lockheed's legendary development program]. I
was Plant Manager in charge of building the SR-71
and the F117 Stealth Fighter before I retired.

Today, Murphy has four kids. One is a Captain in
the Navy. Another is a Colonel in the Air Force. One is
a computer scientist and the other a science and math
teacher.

He remembers too many cases of people dying during
the Cold War. Surrounded by that kind of atmosphere, a
personal sense of doom can begin to grow. Murphy felt
a keen sense of having cheated death and didn't want to
take any more chances on dying young. So he retired in
1986 at age 55 and has enjoyed traveling the world.

One of the trips he took was to Mount Charleston in
2001, organized by the Silent Heroes of the Cold War, to
see the crash site and the rescue mission with the family
members of the victims.

While riding on the bus to get there, "A guy walked
up to me and said 'You Bob Murphy?"

I said, 'Yeah?'"

The man responded with a queer message: *'I have your body bag.'"*

Murphy couldn't help but blurt out: *"Why the hell is that?"*

Murphy went on to ask if he could have it, but immediately Bob's wife shouted out in horror:

What the hell would you want that for?

Epilogue

Bob Murphy says while the accident on top of Mount Charleston on November 17, 1955, did not impact the critical operations of the U-2 project, it did impact Lockheed's relationship with the military, which had ultimate control over the flights. Murphy says Kelly Johnson, the CEO of Lockheed at the time, required that from that day forward (the day of the accident), the company would use its own pilots instead of military ones. The company's pilots would be required to have more than 100,000 hours of flight time under their belts. That's tens of thousands of hours more than Pappas and Winham had. Also, the company would only use its own aircraft.

The fact that Lockheed could call these shots begs the question of whether military aircraft and flight crews were used by the company as a cost-saving measure or if the use of military pilots was mandated for security by the CIA. The question that is never answered is who made that flight path change, military or private interests? That answer is buried deeper than the classified documents. This type of relationship between private and government projects remains in question today: Who's calling the shots in the publicly-funded military? Do private interests ultimately control the purse strings too? Murphy may have the anecdotal answer.

Standing in his small home office in Henderson, Nevada, Murphy likes to point to pictures of all the aircraft he helped develop over the years. One element he didn't have to contend with during the development of the U-2, but one that has become a real pain in the ass for recent developments, is the increased level of bureaucracy we have today, he says. Murphy says today's system of checks on private contractors is one in which every penny and every move by a contractor must be checked and approved by the government or else continued funding for the project is at risk. He's proud that the level of bureaucracy and protocol today didn't exist during the development of the U-2.

To understand the consequences, we take a look back to the time of the development of the U-2, a Wild West of individual mavericks who held the freedom to make educated guesses about the best path to follow on an unlimited budget. That Wild West atmosphere allowed these mavericks to take risks, make quick decisions, and correct mistakes as they arose. Is it that spirit which inspired the unapproved flight path of doomed USAF 9068 on their destination from Burbank? Those consequences ran deep for generations.

Today we know people worked tirelessly during the Cold War to spare countless lives developing the U-2. Undeniably, there have also been casualties from secret wars and weapons development. At least the secrets of one day, November 17, 1955, have now been uncloaked and these forgotten heroes and their dedication to freedom will no longer be lost in obscurity.

NOTES

Knapp, George (2005). Report written by Knapp. "Area 51 Declassified," KLAS-TV, Las Vegas.

Introduction
1 Notes on the Meeting of a Committee to Consider the Feasibility and Conditions for a Preliminary Radiological Safety Shot for Operation. "Windsquall." 1951.

Chapter I: Destination Classified
2 David, D. *The Encyclopedia of Civil Aircraft: Profiles and specifications for civil aircraft from the 1920s to the present day.* Thunder Bay Press: San Diego. 1999.

Chapter IV: Lost History Discovered
3 Hruda, L. E-mail to Steve Ririe. Subject: Silent Heroes of the Cold War National Monument. February 25, 2001.

4 Hruda, L. E-mail to Steve Ririe. Subject: SHCW National Monument. May 8, 2001.

5 Hruda, L. E-mail to Steve Ririe. Subject: SHCW Expedition 2001. June 12, 2001.

6 Kreimendahl, B. E-mail to Steve Ririe. No subject. August 9, 2001.

7 Kreimendahl, B. E-mail to Steve Ririe. No subject. August 9, 2001.

8 Kreimendahl, B. E-mail to Steve Ririe, Subject: SHCW Expedition. June 14, 2001.

9 Rogers, K. "Relatives of plane crash victims make somber trek to wreckage." *Las Vegas Review-Journal.* August 19, 2001.

Chapter V: Silent Heroes of the Cold War
10 Bray, M. James F. Bray Family. E-mail to Marian Kennedy. April 28, 2001.

11 Wolling, S. Personal communication to Steve Ririe. March 25, 2001.

12 Caleela Danley to Steve Ririe. March 14, 2001.

13 Farris, M. E-mail to Marian Kennedy, Subject: Hello Again. July 23, 2001.

14 *Deseret News.* "Nephi Airman Among 14 Killed in crash on high Nevada peak, Funeral Services scheduled for Saturday at 2 p.m. at Nephi Third Ward Chapel." Vol 46, Number 47. November 24, 1955.

15 Bullock, R. Personal communication with Mabel L. Anderson. Ralph E. Bullock, Major 76th Air Transport Squadron. November 23, 1955.

16 *Enterprise*, "Sgt. Gaines' Rites held at 2 p.m. Sunday." Ripley, Tennessee. 1955.

17 Hruda, L. E-mail to Steve Ririe. Subject: SHCW National Monument. February 25, 2001.

18 Marr, S. E-mail to Steve Ririe. No subject. April 16, 2001.

19 Marr, W. E-mail to Steve Ririe. No subject. April 18, 2001.

20 Marr, S. Personal communication with Steve Ririe. April 9, 2001.

21 Larish, J. E-mail to Charles Churchill. January 29, 2001.

22 O'Donnell, T. E-mail to dmjrbrown. Subject: Belated "Thank You" to family of Merle Frehner. May 30, 2001.

23 O'Donnell, T. E-mail to Steve Ririe, Subject: Silent Heroes Weekend. October 11-12, 2002.

24 Reeves, R. Personal communication Promotion Orders. December 13, 1955.

25 Bullock, R. Personal communication to Florence L. Summers. November 23, 1955.

26 *Los Angeles Times,* "Rites Set for Air Crash Victim Harold C. Silent." November 23, 1955.

27 *The Sunday Enterprise,* "Former BHS Hoop Star is Presumed Dead." Brockton, Massachussetts. November 18, 1955.

28 Lyons, K. "Shroud of secrecy lifts from 1955 CIA air crash." *The Sunday Enterprise.* Brockton, Massachusetts, A1. February 11, 2001.

29 *San Antonio Express,* "3 Kelly Airmen Missing, Trio among 14 in plane crash." A1, November 19, 1955.

30 Winham. E-mail from Steve Winham. Subject: Mount Charleston plane crash. 2001.

ABOUT THE AUTHOR

Kyril Plaskon grew up east of San Diego just a few miles from Tecate, Mexico. Spanish was his first formal language, as taught in first through third grades at various barrios in San Diego.

He attended college at the University of Alaska–Fairbanks while living, at times, in a tent and chopping his own wood for heat. An award-winning broadcast and print journalist, Plaskon has worked both abroad and in various US states.

In 1997, he left journalism to manage a rickshaw business in San Diego. That career in transportation was short-lived, returning to journalism three months later. As a border reporter at KPBS-San Diego, he won several Society of Professional Journalist's top awards in 2001, including Best of Show for exposing child sex tourism in Tijuana, Mexico. He has won awards also for covering cross-border electricity and pollution issues during the energy crisis.

Today, he is pursuing his master's degree in journalism at UNLV and building a home at the base of Mount Charleston.

Plaskon is a member of the Lee Canyon Ski Patrol and enjoys participating in triathlons. He resides in Las Vegas with wife, Mina and daughter Alara.